The Day Trader's ADVANTAGE

How To Move

from One

Winning Position

to the Next

Howard Abell

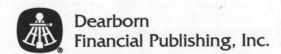

Dearborn
Financial Publishing, Inc.

Acquisitions Editor: Christine E. Litavsky
Managing Editor: Jack Kiburz
Project Editor: Karen A. Christensen
Cover Design: S. Laird Jenkins Corporation
Interior Design: Lucy Jenkins

©1996 by Innergame Partners

Published by Dearborn Financial Publishing, Inc.®

Printed in the United States of America

96 97 98 10 9 8 7 6 5 4 3 2 1

Library of Congress Cataloging-in-Publication Data

Abell, Howard.
  The day trader's advantage : how to move from one winning position
    to the next / Howard Abell.
      p.   cm.
  Includes index.
  ISBN 0-7931-1778-X
  1. Futures.   2. Commodity futures.   3. Financial futures.
  I. Title.
  HG6024.A3A24   1996
  332.64'5—dc20   96-11551
                                                      CIP

Dedication

I would like to dedicate this book to all the traders who have the courage to successfully pursue their goal.

CONTENTS

Twenty years ago a novice trader walked onto the floor of the world's largest financial futures exchange armed with an Ivy League education, a knowledge of the fundamental and technical factors that drive markets, a burning desire to succeed and a small trading account. It was not enough. Knowledge, determination and capital alone when trading stocks or futures are not the recipe for instant success. There are no holy grails, secret elixirs or magic bullets in trading. The undeniable truth is that successful trading requires an ongoing commitment to hold a mirror unflinchingly to one's self. It is a relentlessly challenging exercise in self-analysis and realization. In my experience, the traders who don't make it confuse self-deception with self-discovery. They always have an excuse to explain why trades don't work out, as if they were the victims of some shadowy perpetrator: their broker, the fill, the chairman of the Fed or some other external felon, never themselves!

The key to successful trading always resides in the development and fulfillment of our own personal characteristics: patience, judgment, courage, intellect and certainty. Add to this mix discipline, focus, optimism and the confidence to be fully prepared to do battle in the cerebral thunderdome of psychological warfare. Negativity and debilitating emotions are the *real* enemies in trading. Like gorillas in the mist, they reveal themselves at just the wrong moments. No matter how good your trading system or how strong your will to succeed at trading, technical analysis will never provide you with the psychological capability to overcome adversity, fight negative impulses or control disempowering emotions. True trading mastery derives from understanding the relatively small role technical analytical factors play in the overall trading process and the inestimably important role that correct market attitudes and beliefs exert in facilitating a consistently profitable result.

Twenty years ago the novice trader referred to earlier had the good fortune to meet Howard Abell. Howard got me started on the right path, and for this I am forever in his debt. It was just the insights above that he generously shared with me. I remember vividly Howard's image of the traders who get lost studying technical analysis without developing the appropriate attitudes. He referred to them as trading gerbils going round and round on a spinning wheel of technical indicators in an endless and never-to-be-realized search for the perfect system.

When I first met Howard, he had already cultivated a national reputation, with his partner, George Segal, as one of the most successful commodity traders on the exchange. Over many years I have seen him operate on both the trading floor and in front of a computer screen with surgical precision and timing, always with grace under fire.

I am honored that Howard has asked me to write the foreword for *The Day Trader's Advantage* for two reasons. First, I know he could easily have asked any one of a number of other prominent traders who would have surely agreed to do it in a heartbeat. Second, and more importantly, it is a privilege to endorse the fine work of someone I have known so well for such a long time. I think this book may well be the first book written by a trader of Howard's caliber that reveals in full his trading method, the approach he uses day in and day out to trade markets successfully.

There will be those who upon learning of Howard's successful trading methodology will say to themselves incredulously, "Is that all? It couldn't possibly be that simple!" To the many other traders who read *The Day Trader's Advantage* and really get "it," recognizing the obvious profundity of the Innergame approach, I wish you all the success and fulfillment that is possible in trading.

Bob Koppel

An old southern saying goes like this: "The best fertilizer is the farmer's shadow." This adage applies equally well to trading as it docs to farming. Trading profits are cultivated in the rich soil of market discipline, strict money management and consistent adherence to a proven trading strategy.

No day trading system is perfect; however, the use of one is critical for trading success. To be successful, a day trading system must be profitable, consistent and personal. In short, it must be guided by an overriding and all-encompassing trading strategy that takes into account the real-time characteristics of dynamic markets.

To the best of my knowledge, to date, nowhere in the investment literature has anyone presented a profitable method for day trading the market, futures or equities, that takes into consideration the invariable daily trading context: inconclusive and conflicting market information, debilitating emotions and ambiguous technical indicators.

How does the trader create a real-time profitable day trading strategy that conforms to the unique psychological and methodological needs of the individual? Historically, books on day trading offer either a survey of systems and indicators that may be used for day trading or a specific system that is presented in the abstract, a hypothetical offering at best. When the psychology of the trader is introduced into the discussion, it is typically mentioned in passing or as a theoretical construct rather than as an underlying and integral aspect of any winning system.

The Day Trader's Advantage: How To Move from One Winning Position to the Next addresses all of the above considerations in detail; it is based on 25 years of personal day trading success, intimate knowledge of the psychology underlying successful trading based on my previous publications, *The Innergame of Trading* (Irwin, 1993) and *The Outer Game of Trading* (Irwin, 1994), my personal work training successful traders on and off the exchange floors as a principal of a clearing firm specializing in our own proprietary traders, as well as interviews with literally hundreds of successful day traders.

I believe *The Day Trader's Advantage* builds logically on the insights of my two previous books, coauthored with Bob Koppel, and will provide an invaluable resource for traders to significantly strengthen their market performance.

Howard Abell

ACKNOWLEDGMENTS

Many people's contributions made writing *The Day Trader's Advantage* a deeply rewarding experience. Among them are David Silverman, Robin Mesch, Bill Williams, Larry Rosenberg, Toby Crabel and Mei Ping Yang. The success of this book is a testament to their outstanding talents and fertile minds. In particular, I wish to thank Bob Koppel, friend and business partner, whose market insights prove invaluable day in and day out. Bob is a living testament to the "Innergame" trading method.

I wish to thank Roslyn Kolin Abell, wife and friend, for her important insights to the systems portion of the Innergame approach and for her strong support throughout the years.

Finally, I would like to thank Christine Litavsky and the entire staff at Dearborn Financial Publishing; their ongoing commitment to and enthusiasm for this project are gladly acknowledged.

"It is the mind that maketh good or ill, that maketh wretch or happy, rich or poor."

Edmund Spenser

PART ONE

Psychological and Strategic Considerations

CHAPTER 1

The Psychology of Successful Day Trading

"Successful traders share a surprisingly large number of attitudes in regards to why they do it. For example, almost all claim that they do not trade for the money, but view the market as a difficult game that is constantly changing. They are by now rich and diversified enough to afford this attitude."

Stanley W. Angrist
The Wall Street Journal

If you turn to almost any book on trading, you will see some or all of the following trading axioms.

- Buy low, sell high.
- Manage your money well.
- Don't overtrade.
- Don't turn a profit into a loss.
- The trend is your friend.
- Learn how to use orders properly.
- Don't add to a loss.
- Take big profits.
- Take small losses.
- Avoid the crowd.

- Buy the rumor, sell the fact.
- The market is always right.
- Avoid fear and greed.
- Trade liquid markets.
- Don't buy or sell price alone.
- Preserve capital.

There are others, of course, and almost everyone knows these trading axioms. Yet the basic question remains: Why are not more investors and traders achieving the results that they desire from the market?

My goal in *The Day Trader's Advantage* is to place a spotlight on how winning traders think, the specific characteristics of thought and action held in common that set apart the world's most successful traders. I'll also try to answer two questions: (1) How important to trading success are hard work, skill, discipline, patience and confidence? And (2) most important of all, how can traders take advantage of these insights in order to formulate consistently rewarding short-term trading strategies for a real-time day trading plan?

Basic Strategies for Short-Term Trading of Markets

In essence, there are only a few basic strategies for short-term trading of markets. They include but are not limited to the following:

- Scalping
- Day trading
- Spreading

Scalping

On the futures trading floor, scalpers are the equivalent of market makers in the securities world, although, unlike securities traders, they are under no obligation to make markets. Their main focus is to make small profits by carefully calculating surgical attacks in order to capture small price changes on each transaction. Scalpers limit their exposure by moving quickly with a closely defined risk that, given their short-term perspective, also limits their profit potential.

Whether conducted on or off the floor, this method is based primarily on volume rather than on large profit potential on any given trade.

Day Trading (Conventional)

The day trader's focus is more long term than the scalper's. Day traders seek to identify pivotal points in the market's daily action. They search for entry points based on perceived buying and selling climaxes, retracements, trend line pull-backs and the like. Their risks are close and well-defined but with increased upside potential because they are looking for critical daily turns that may materialize into longer market moves. Typically, the position is liquidated at the end of the trading session, a strategy that does not allow for the exposure or opportunity of an open overnight position.

Day Trading (Innergame Swing Trading Approach)

Swing traders' time horizon may extend anywhere from one to five days. Their trading is supported by a well-formulated calculation based on price level, history or market economics that may be arrived at by either a fundamental or technical bias or a combination of the two. Swing traders will stay with their bias until market dynamics

---

FIGURE 1.1   Most Common Types of Spread Positions

Strategy	Example Trade
Intracommodity spread	Long March '95 Eurodollars
	Short June '96 Eurodollars
Intercommodity spread	Long gold, short silver
Intermarket spread	Long CBOT wheat, short KCBOT wheat

---

have aligned measurably, targeted price levels have been reached or fundamental conditions have changed. Of necessity, greater risk exists in swing trading, although it is still well calculated and highly defined. Of course, profit potential accordingly is also greatly increased given the expansion of perspective. Swing trading enjoys all the advantages of conventional day trading plus the profit potential of overnight positioning.

Spreading

Spreaders can be scalpers, day traders or swing traders. The techniques they utilize, however, are substantially different from those of outright traders. Spreaders focus on the differential, that is, the difference in price between one futures contract month and another contract month, or the difference in prices between related markets (e.g., corn and wheat, gold and silver, Eurodollars and bonds). Although successful spreading strategies always involve good risk management, the unlimited possibilities create widely varying risk/reward ratios. (See Figure 1.1.)

The Skills of the Successful Trader

In his autobiography *Baruch: My Own Story* (Holt, Rinehart and Winston, 1957), the legendary entrepreneur, Bernard Baruch, offers ten rules for successful speculation.

1. Don't speculate unless you do it full time.

2. Resist so-called inside information or tips.

3. Before purchasing a security, know everything you can find out about a company: its earning and its capacity for growth.

4. Never attempt to buy a bottom or sell a top of a market: "This is a feat only achieved by liars."

5. Take your losses swiftly and clearly; the first loss is your easiest loss.

6. Don't buy too many securities; focus on a few investments that can be monitored carefully.

7. Periodically reappraise all your investments to make sure they are appropriate to your particular strategy.

8. Know when you can sell to your greatest advantage (also applies to buying, of course).

9. Never invest all your funds; keep liquid.

10. Don't try to be a jack-of-all-investments; stick to the field you know best.

Source: Reprinted with permission of Henry Holt and Co., Inc.

Baruch, a lifelong skeptic of both giving and taking advice, qualified his rules of sound speculation with this caveat: "Being so skeptical about the usefulness of advice, I have been reluctant to lay down any rules or guidelines on how to invest or speculate wisely. Still, there are a number of things I have learned from my own experience which might be worth listing for those who are able to muster the necessary self-discipline." And, of course, isn't that the essence of it? All rules of sound investment begin and end with the adoption and mastery of specific psychological skills that successful trading requires.

Day trading, in particular because of the very nature of short-term trading, forces us to sink or swim in our own psychology. It is the concentrated time frame of split-second decision making within a context, perhaps barrage is a better word, of conflicting and contradictory data that makes it seem at times impossible!

Not so.

In my experience, day trading can be enormously rewarding both psychologically and financially. But only if the right attitudes are put in place and the necessary psychological skills are mastered.

> "He who knows much about others may be learned, but he who understands himself is more intelligent. He who controls others may be more powerful, but he who has mastered himself is mightier still."
>
> Lao-Tse
> Chinese Philosopher

FIGURE 1.2 The Psychological Skills Necessary To Become a Successful Day Trader

---

- Compelling personal motivation
- Goal setting
- Confidence

- Anxiety control
- Focus
- State of mind management

8

FIGURE 1.3   The Importance of Day Trading Goals

Goal	Benefit	Trading Behavior
Performance goal	Focuses on improvement in relation to your own standards.	Increases physical and psychological skills related to trading.
Outcome goal	Helps determine what's important to you.	Develop techniques and strategies that match trader's personality.
Motivation goal	Helps increase effort; directs attention.	Increases trader's enthusiasm and confidence.

Psychological Skills of a Successful Day Trader

Certain psychological skills need to be identified, learned and practiced to achieve success in day trading. They are listed in Figure 1.2 and explained in detail on the previous page.

Compelling Personal Motivation

Compelling motivation involves possessing the intensity to do whatever it takes to win at trading: to overcome a bad day or a temporary setback in the market to achieve your trading goals. It also means sticking to your trading plan and not allowing a momentary impulse based on fear and greed to control your decisions. Many day traders live and die on a roller coaster of inhibiting emotion. This is not the soil in which effective trading flowers.

Goal Setting

Goal setting is key for traders. It focuses traders on what is important in terms of motivation, outcome and mechanics. Goals give direction and focus to the trading plan as well. You must know what you are trying to accomplish

---

FIGURE 1.4 Operational Definitions of Day Trading Goals

- Specific—clear, precise, well-defined
- Time framed—stated within a specific time period
- Positive—stated in a way that is empowering
- Controlled—completely within your command
- Realistic—not necessary to become the next George Soros, which was George's goal
- Measurable—easily quantifiable

---

if you want to achieve an excellent trading result. You must be able to answer without qualification: Am I scalping, day trading or swing trading? Is my time frame 5 minutes, 30 minutes or 5 days? Then act accordingly. Goal setting allows you to make decisions without hesitation or ambiguity. Figure 1.3 outlines the importance and reasons behind setting trading goals.

When setting goals, ask yourself the following questions:

- Do I have in writing a clearly defined set of trading goals?

- Have I specifically done something to move me closer to achieving my goals?

- Do I have a clear idea of what I want to accomplish right now in the market?

- Do I concentrate on goals rather than procedures?

- Do I evaluate my progress based on accomplishment rather than activity?

As you think about your trading goals, remember that they should satisfy the criteria listed in Figure 1.4.

FIGURE 1.5   Sources of Day Trading Anxiety

Anxiety	Manifestation	Solution
Fear of Failure	Trader feels intense pressure to perform, ties self-worth to trading, becomes a perfectionist, or is overly concerned about what others think.	Focus on applying your methodology and mentally rehearse the mechanics of the trade. Also rehearse the attitude in your mind that trading is not about proving anything to anybody. The closer you can get to focusing on your methodology the more you will feel in control of this anxiety.
Fear of Success	Trader loses control or engages in "euphoric" trading. Trader doubts himself or herself.	If your day trading approach has shown statistical reliability in its performance, rehearse feelings of confidence as you mentally run through the placement, management and closing out of the trade. Feel in a literal sense how you personally experience confidence.
Loss of Control	Trader feels market is out to get him or her. (It's not!) Trader loses sense of personal responsibility when trading.	Teach yourself how to get into a physically and psychologically relaxed state when trading. Focus on your specific methodology and expect small losses!

In my experience from training my own proprietary traders, I have found that traders abandon their goals for many reasons, among them: self-limiting beliefs, an unresourceful state of mind, ill-defined personal trading strategy and lack of physical and psychological energy.

The answer to overcoming these trading obstacles always resides in psychological rather than technical analysis—but of course you already know this.

Confidence

When I speak of confidence, I am not referring to cockiness, euphoria or arrogance. Overconfidence in trading is lethal. Confidence, on the other hand, is essential and is the trader's natural expression of self-trust and of being in control. Confidence is the mental state of effortlessly expecting a good result based on hard work, discipline and an effective (tested and proven) methodology.

Anxiety Control

Sometimes I think anxiety was invented just for trading! Traders have to confront and master so many anxieties to be effective and apply their proven strategy. Figure 1.5 explains the most common anxieties, how they reveal themselves and their antidotes.

Focus

Figure 1.6 reveals graphically the focus that is necessary for successful day trading results.

State of Mind Management

To be successful at day trading you must constantly trade from a state of mind that allows you to maintain a

---

FIGURE 1.6   The Successful Day Trader's Focus

Well-analyzed ⟶   Automatic execution ⟶   Successful day trading
  and strategized   (based on highly   results (whether the
  trade (based on   concentrated focus   trade makes or loses
  probability)   and confidence)   money)

---

high level of self-esteem, unshakable confidence and laser straight focus. This state of mind is characterized by being relaxed, centered, anxiety free, self-trusting and resourceful. See Figure 1.7.

A positive state of mind is the result of consistently processing positive verbal attitudes, beliefs and images that will enhance your trading performance. Here are a few things to keep in mind.

- Expect the best of yourself.

- Establish a personal standard of excellence.

- Create an internal atmosphere for success based on visual, auditory and feeling (kinesthetic) imagery that enhances performance.

- Communicate positively and effectively with yourself. See yourself as positive, resourceful and self-empowering.

FIGURE 1.7   The Successful Day Trader's State of Mind

Positive State of ⟶   Allows for the ⟶   Positive trading result
  Mind   unhesitating
                         implementation of
                         one's trading
                         strategy.

FIGURE 1.8   The Syntax of Successful Day Trading

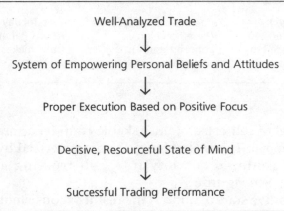

Well-Analyzed Trade

↓

System of Empowering Personal Beliefs and Attitudes

↓

Proper Execution Based on Positive Focus

↓

Decisive, Resourceful State of Mind

↓

Successful Trading Performance

- Rehearse a system of personal beliefs that can enhance your state immediately.

The psychological skills necessary to day trade successfully require ongoing commitment and conditioning. You must practice them day in and day out. I have been keeping up-to-date charts by hand in over 20 different commodities for over 25 years. Technical analysis is very important. It is not, however, in my opinion, as important as working through the psychological and attitudinal issues of trading in general and day trading in particular. The complete process for successful day trading is sketched out in Figure 1.8.

"You learn to distinguish the good traders from the bad, the successful techniques from the unsuccessful, and the good habits from the faulty. You also learn to distinguish the lover from the fighter, the winners from the losers, the serious from the frivolous, the cerebral from the superficial, and the friend from the foe. But above all, you learn that the psychological makeup of the trader is the single most critical element of success."

Leo Melamed
Leo Melamed on the Markets

CHAPTER 2

Overcoming the Psychological Barriers That Hold Most Day Traders Back

I have yet to meet a paper trader who consistently lost money. It's a funny thing, but they all make a financial killing! My partner, Bob Koppel, when speaking at trading conferences invariably is confronted during his presentation by one of these traders (usually a doctor or lawyer) who argue with Bob for placing so much "unnecessary" importance on the psychological aspects of trading. Bob usually takes this all in good humor, reminds his interrogator that he is not promulgating some new age "science" but merely sharing with the audience essential issues key to his own development as a trader. He adds also that this perspective is reaffirmed by the interviews we have conducted with many of the world's top traders. The interesting thing is that Bob always tells them that if they are truly committed to becoming serious traders, he will be looking forward to their call in the future.

FIGURE 2.1   The Essential Psychological Barriers to Successful Day
Trading

- Not defining a loss
- Not taking a loss or profit
- Getting locked into a belief
- Trading on "inside information" or taking a tip
- Kamikaze trading
- Euphoric trading
- Hesitating at your numbers
- Not catching a breakout
- Not focusing on opportunities
- Being more invested in being right than in making money
- Trying to be perfect
- Not consistently applying your trading system
- Not having a well-defined money management system
- Not being in the right state of mind

Sure enough, six months pass and Bob gets "the call." It often goes something like this: "Mr. Koppel, I'm a basket case. I've got this great trading system, but . . ."

I'll spare the details; you get the point!

Barriers to Successful Day Trading

Specific psychological barriers need to be addressed when day trading. These barriers are listed in Figure 2.1 and discussed in detail in this chapter.

Not Defining a Loss

No one day trades expecting to lose. No one buys thinking the market will break, and conversely, no one sells assuming the market is about to rally to new highs. But to paraphrase a famous saying: "Things happen!" Day traders must identify without qualification their loss point *before*, not after, entering the trade. When you get stopped out, just pick yourself up, dust yourself off and start all over again.

Look both ways before you cross the street! I've heard it a million times, but you know what? I almost got hit by a car the other day. I was walking across Franklin Street, talking on the telephone with a trader upstairs, and I didn't notice that the stoplight had changed. A car just came down off [a parking garage] ramp, honked his horn and missed me by about two feet. It scared the hell out of me! My little four-year-old nephew said, "Uncle Tony, stop, look and listen!" It's a cliche, right? But how many traders follow that market truth?

Tony Saliba
Market Wizard

Not Taking a Loss or Profit

Each day trade should have its own internal logic, based on probability, and it should be consistent with your own methodology. When the market has moved to your exit point either on the upside or downside, you must react automatically, without hesitation. You must take the profit or loss. If the market continues to move in your direction once again, based on probability and consistent with your technical bias, find a new entry point. Reentry is an essential element in any trading system. When the market does give you profit, I believe it is essential that you take it. It is psychologically important that you walk away from the trade with change in your pocket.

Getting Locked into a Belief

It is so easy to get locked into this jail cell of personal opinion. The market does not lie; it reveals all to the keen observer. You must not confuse your subjective opinion with the objective action of the market. Remember, the market feels no obligation to gratify *your* opinion! Day traders need to focus on a single rigorous method that works; all else is just another opinion. Money talks; all else walks.

Trading on Inside Information or Taking a Tip

Inside information is for losers only! By the time you've heard it, it has circulated widely. If you don't enjoy playing the role of salami entering the slicer, don't day trade on someone else's tip. Typically, this information comes from the phone-people or trading desks. They will tell you that if the market gets below a certain level, the floor will start buying or selling. If they were so smart, they'd be in the ring carding trades, not manning the phones!

Kamikaze Trading

What more can I say? Crashing airplanes don't fly! If you feel angry, betrayed, in need of revenge, apply to law school. Do not trade; you will crash land!

Euphoric Trading

Euphoric trading is the opposite of kamikaze trading. You're feeling invincible, heroic, bulletproof. You feel the lottery can't help but draw your ticket. As soon as you lose your objectivity, bullets start piercing flesh!

Hesitating at Your Numbers

Day traders do not have the luxury of hesitating once they have identified a setup trade. It is both financially and psychologically debilitating not to pick up the ball and run. The discipline always must be to take the trades that are consistent with your methodology, no matter what! If you take the trade and get stopped out, welcome to the world of day trading. Remember, you can't score touchdowns without the ball.

Not Catching a Breakout

Refusing to take advantage of a breakout is another form of hesitation. It is like going to the airport and watching the planes take off. Wouldn't it be fun just once to get on board and arrive at an exciting destination?

Not Focusing on Opportunities

You will encounter many (constant and consistent) distractions in the market. So much of day trading is just having the ability to get beyond the noise, the talk and the smoke! Consistency to your approach with a high degree of confidence and optimism will keep your focus clear. You must find a way to get beyond all the head fakes!

Being More Invested in Being Right Than in Making Money

Is your goal to become an analyst or a trader? You must answer that question. If your technical analysis is turning you into a Ph.D. in the S&P, join a university faculty. You'll save money! Trading is not about scholarship. It's about making money. That is not to say that money should be the object of all efforts. I believe it shouldn't. But this is one game where the scorecard is tallied in hard currency. It is not enough to point out that you had the high or low of the market!

I know it may sound strange to many readers, but there is an inverse relationship between analysis and trading results. More analysis or being able to make more distinctions in the market's behavior will not produce better trading results. There are many traders who find themselves caught in this exasperating loop, thinking that more or better analysis is going to give them the confidence they need to do what needs to be done to achieve success. It's what I call a trading paradox that most traders find difficult, if not impossible to reconcile, until they realize you can't use analysis to overcome your fear of being wrong or losing money. It just doesn't work!

Mark Douglas
The Outer Game of Trading

Trying To Be Perfect

You don't have to be perfect, merely excellent! Excellence produces results; perfection produces ulcers!

Not Consistently Applying Your Trading System

Your trading system is there for one purpose only: to be used so that you can garner profits, letting them pile up like pleasing snow drifts!

Not Having a Well-Defined Money Management Program

Literally hundreds of books are written on money management. You don't have to read them! For day trading purposes, your trade should give you a minimum of a 2:1 risk-to-reward ratio.

Not Being in the Right State of Mind

Funny, but it comes back to state of mind. In my experience, over 90 percent of all trading failure is the result of not being in the right state of mind. The right state of mind produces the right results!

> It is our belief that continually elevating your state of mind by focusing on internal and external phenomena that allow you to stay resourceful and true to your trading strategy is the answer. We have demonstrated how to do this through processing positive beliefs and thoughts and by directing your physiology. When a negative thought comes into consciousness and begins to distract your focus, don't fight it. Acknowledge its existence and go forward.
>
> Koppel and Abell
> *The Innergame of Trading*

Successful trading, in essence, comes down to this: Formulate a day trading plan that works, overcome your own personal psychological barriers and condition yourself to produce feelings of self trust, high self-esteem and unshakable conviction and confidence. Doing this naturally leads to good judgment and winning trades with a proven methodology, based on probability.

What Gives You the Edge in Day Trading?

The edge that makes the difference in day trading comes down to this:

1. *Fully understand your motive for trading.* Once you know what your motives are, examine them carefully. Most traders trade in a constant state of conflict. My experience reveals that many people who think they want to day trade really don't.

2. *Develop a personal strategy that works for you and fits your personality.* If the system you're using doesn't feel right, you're going to lose before you even start. Remember, by the very nature of day trading, you must trade a system that is totally within your control.

3. *It has to be fun.* I can't stress this point enough. Trading has to literally feel good. You must be in a frame of mind that allows you to enjoy the process effortlessly, be resourceful and make good judgments, even when you are losing! You don't have to like losing, but you do have to have a sense of humor.

4. *Hard work is essential.* There's no way to get around it. You must put in the time. As Thomas Edison said, "A lot of people do not recognize opportunity because it usually goes around wearing overalls, looking like hard work."

5. *Confidence.* You must possess a repertoire of personal beliefs that constantly reinforces feelings of high self-esteem and confidence in your analysis and execution of trades, again, whether you win or lose. Needless to say, discipline, patience, personal responsibility and repeated success in day trading make this a lot easier.

6. *Positive state of mind.* All top-performing traders have developed an internal mental terrain that reduces anxiety and promotes excellence. They manage to achieve this end by internally representing external events in such a way that assures success, adjusting and redefining as they deem appropriate. They do this by employing a belief system that does not allow for the concept of failure and a personal focus that concentrates on what is essential to achieving this end. In short, they have

---

FIGURE 2.2 Critical Factors in Determining the Edge That Makes the Difference in Day Trading

---

Trader Response	Having the Edge	Losing the Edge
Patience	Waits for opportunities to materialize based on well-thought-out game plan.	Plans very little; reacts according to personal whim.
Discipline	Sees the big picture; responds deliberately.	Is emotional, anxious and often confused about what to do.
Strategy	Plans carefully; limits losses; lets profits run.	Plans little or not at all; does not rely on consistent methodology.
Expertise	Is well-prepared; has done the necessary homework.	Knows little about market; is unprepared.
Motive	Has long-term motive, e.g., intellectual challenge.	Wants to make money; wants instant gratification.
Goals	Defines goals clearly.	Has ill-defined goals.
Risk control	Wants highly controlled risk/reward ratio.	Knows little or no control over risk/reward ratio.
State of mind	Has positive, resourceful empowering beliefs and focus. Has high level of self-esteem and trust; is relaxed and confident.	Is nervous, anxious; believes the worst will happen. Focus is distracted; trades in conflict.

---

mastered the ability to create states of mind and body that are resourceful and that assure whatever it takes to succeed. See Figure 2.2 for a condensation of the key qualities that give you the edge in day trading.

You must spend the time—you must study the characteristics of successful traders. You must study your own mistakes. You must study the mistakes of the others around you. Increasing levels of sophistication will put you in the direction of understanding who you are. You must really study your own self and understand what you're all about. It's not clear to me whether I didn't do this whole thing backwards where I studied the economics and science of trading and worked into the psychology of trading and finally got involved in some sort of philosophical thinking of the whole trading process. It's not clear to me that I didn't do the whole thing backwards and shouldn't have studied philosophy and psychology at the start and it might have made the whole process easier.

Jeffrey Silverman
The Innergame of Trading

CHAPTER 3

Strategy and the Overall Game Plan

*"All men can see those tactics whereby I conquer,
but what none can see is the strategy out of
which victory is evolved."*

Sun-Tzu
The Art of War

It is important as day traders to be able to distinguish the difference between trading strategy and trading tactics.

Strategy is the process of determining your major trading goals and then adopting a course of action whereby you allocate the resources necessary to achieve those goals. Trading tactics is the process of translating broad strategic goals into specific objectives that are relevant to a single component of your trading plan.

In Part II, I discuss my own personal day trading system, The Innergame Swing Trading Method of Short-Term Trading. I will focus on specific tactics and technical analytical considerations. However, to lay a framework for the strategic context of its application, I will concentrate here on what I believe are the essential elements of a successful day trading strategy that underly all tactical applications.

The Essentials of Successful Day Trading

Successful day trading is based on a number of essential elements, which are listed in Figure 3.1 and explained in detail in this chapter.

Assumes Personal Responsibility for All Market Actions

Traders often say they "make a profit" but "take a loss." The reality, of course, is that *we* make both. You the trader produce the results. This fact may seem obvious. However, I can assure you—based on my 25 years of experience, and having worked with hundreds of traders—that it is the rare trader who truly lives by this credo!

> It isn't your broker, your brother-in-law, the chairman of the board of the Fed, the fill, the computer, the unemployment report—it is you! It's a simple fact that must be understood in the adoption of any trading strategy: You are responsible for the results. Good or bad, the buck stops (and starts) here!
>
> Koppel and Abell
> *The Outer Game of Trading*

Takes into Consideration Your Motivation For Trading

Your day trading approach must take into consideration your motivation for trading. In addition, your method must feel "right." To feel right, it must be consistent and congruent with your personality. If it doesn't feel natural, it is like taking a ten-mile hike in boots that are two sizes too small. Ask yourself exactly why you want to day trade. Is your personality and approach suitable to the task?

FIGURE 3.1   The Essential Elements of a Successful Day Trading
Strategy

- Assumes personal responsibility for all market actions.
- Takes into consideration your motivation for trading.
- Establishes a clear, precise plan of action.
- Creates a point of focus.
- Is automatic and effortless in its implementation.
- Manages risk and assumes losses.
- Allows for patience.
- Has a practical orientation—profit oriented.
- Allows you to produce consistent results.

Establishes a Clear, Precise Plan of Action

The recipe for success in trading is a simple one. Your plan of action needs only three elements:

1. It identifies a signal (opportunity).

2. It allows you to take immediate action (buy or sell).

3. It allows you to feel good no matter what the result as long as the trade is consistent with your specific method or technical bias and is based on probability.

Most day traders, however, experience hesitation or doubt just at the moment of action. To overcome this, you must have a crystal clear point of focus that allows you to resolve the omnipresent internal and external hindrances.

Creates a Point of Focus

Staying fixed on your particular approach, method or system will allow you to resolve all the debilitating emotions you experience while day trading. Establishing the discipline to refocus on your particular method, numbers, system, etc., helps you resolve your natural feelings of anxiety as you are experiencing them. I will talk more about this later when I discuss the application of the Innergame Swing Trading Method. For now the essential point is that you must know what you are looking for and what you are looking at in the market. You must be able to distinguish the signal from the noise and high probability from low probability trades.

Is Automatic and Effortless in Its Implementation

All your hard work as a trader pays off by being able to act automatically and effortlessly in the market when you have a high probability signal. The discipline is to hardwire your neurological system to act at just these times. By being in a position to "catch" those trades, you will find that the need to tell colleagues about the great trades that got away will be greatly neutralized!

Manages Risk and Assumes Losses

All traders take losses. You can't be afraid to lose. Truly, I love the market to take me out and hit my day trading stops. I challenge it to do no less. Do I like to lose? NO! But if the market takes me out, I have paid for some very valuable information. Of course, it goes without saying that my losses are always circumscribed.

Allows for Patience

Following your signal religiously teaches you to have patience and to avoid getting caught up in the minute-to-minute emotions of day trading. Success here means giving yourself the time to make decisions that are based on thoughtful process, method and strategy rather than re-acting to the exciting emotional gyrations of the market.

There are certain characteristics of a mindset that I believe are essential to creating success in the markets or creating consistency. To me, success as a trader is con-sistency. There is an often-used saying on the floor of the exchanges that 'traders just rent their winnings.' As you know, there are many traders who have reached the stage of development where they can put together a substantial string of winning trades for days, weeks or even months, only to lose all or most all of their hard-won equity in a few trades and then start the process all over again. If a trader hasn't neutralized his suscepti-bility to give his winnings back to the market, then he is not what I define as a successful trader.

Mark Douglas
The Outer Game of Trading

Has Practical Orientation—Profit Oriented

Many day traders get bogged down in the theoretical accuracy of their particular system. Accuracy is not neces-sarily important. What is important is performance. Making money supersedes theoretical attachment to a par-ticular ideological or technical bias. Winston Churchill said it best: "It is a socialist idea that making profits is a vice; I consider the real vice is making losses."

Allows You To Produce Consistent Results

Although you can never really have certainty in trading, paradoxically, in order to operate effectively, you must act with certainty. You must act decisively at the point of decision. Consistency in day trading derives from applying a proven method without fail every time a signal is generated. Your trading system provides the organization that allows you to identify and exploit opportunities and achieve consistent results. It goes without saying, the rest is up to you!

The difference between those who succeed and those who fail isn't what they have—It's what they choose to see and do with their resources and their experiences of life.

Anthony Robbins

Your trading strategy should allow you to open your eyes and see market opportunities . . . so that you can act!

Koppel and Abell
The Outer Game of Trading

PART TWO

Technical Analysis and Day Trading

CHAPTER 4

Market Analysis and Day Trading

"The trading system gives the trader the ability to control his or her emotional states rather than allowing them to control him. A system is a disciplined method for organizing dynamic, ever-changing market phenomena."

Koppel and Abell
The Innergame of Trading

Short-term trading telescopes all market movement and behavior into a self-imposed time requirement that enlarges and distorts the impact of the market on the trader's emotional makeup and state of mind. Therefore, day or swing trading demands organization of thought, discipline of action and commitment to make numerous trading decisions in the face of taking repeated losses in the market.

Jerry Jones, the flamboyant owner of the Dallas Cowboys football team, made his fortune in oil and gas. In answer to a question about his successful style, he recounted his early days of wildcatting. "When that telephone rings at two in the morning, you never know if the news is a strike or a dry hole that just cost you a million dollars. More often than not the news of a dry hole is followed by another phone call requiring you to commit to another project whose outcome you won't know for many months. It takes tenacity and a belief in yourself to move on."

FIGURE 4.1 Technical Requirements for Successful Day Trading

- Trend identification
- Market entry point
- Market exit point
- Money management

Successful traders will resonate to this advice; would-be successful traders must learn its lesson!

All the successful traders interviewed for this book possess this ability. Although their methods or systems are different, their approach and state of mind are remarkably similar.

Technical Requirements Needed for Successful Day Trading

The necessary technical ingredients for a successful approach to day or swing trading are shown in Figure 4.1 and described in this chapter.

Trend Identification

What, you are asking? Identify a trend in a day trading system? You bet! Markets exhibit consistent characteristics in up trending, down trending or sideways moves. For example, it's almost axiomatic that buying lower openings in a bull market is a high probability trade. So too is selling higher openings in a bear market.

Trend, however, has many time frames, and the day trader can incorporate and capitalize on each one that can be identified. I like to break trend down to three workable areas: (1) the intermediate-term trend, which is usually three to ten days and is derived from what most traders see as the long-term trend of the market; (2) the short-term trend, which lasts from two to five days and can be in the direction of the intermediate-term trend or a reaction to it;

and (3) the daily trend, which can be the result of the prior day or two setup or an overnight news event or morning government report.

In my proprietary trading system, I have honed the number of computer-generated numbers to just a few that I use to identify the various trends in each time frame and that also create support and resistance within those time frames to trade against. I believe strongly in the KISS (keep it simple, stupid) philosophy of trading. The simpler the better. So now that we have determined our trend in each time frame, we must decide on "entry."

Market Entry Point

Being without a plan of action, that is, without knowing where the market is in relation to where it has been, increases the tendency of reacting to the emotions of the market and getting caught up in the crowd. In simple terms, this running with the herd often results in buying the highs and selling the lows—a common, painful experience!

In short-time-frame trading, efficient entry can be the difference between a missed market, a smaller profit or a larger than necessary loss. By planning several potential scenarios that fit into your system, you prepare yourself for opportunities that the market offers. The most difficult thing for most novice traders to do is to buy the market as it comes crashing down to your point, number or area. Planning and a conviction in your proven method will put you into the market. Buying a hard break or selling a sharp rally to your preplanned point is usually the smallest risk trade you can make. This applies also for buying or selling a breakout. You generally know right away if your buy or sell is a good one, and if not, it usually has the least dollar risk attached to it.

Personally, I try to determine if the market is set up to buy a break, sell a rally or, if it is in a breakout mode, to follow strength or weakness. I then place entry orders in anticipation. This requires patience.

Many times day trading appears like running for a crowded elevator whose doors are just beginning to close. Forget it! Remember another one will be along in a minute. It is important to get into the elevator that will arrive at your floor. Now that leads us to our trading "exit."

Market Exit Point

Steve Conners, the investment adviser and author of *Confessions of a Hedge Fund Manager*, said it well: "I want my stop hit!" He emphasized this point by trailing his stops on profitable trades so close to the market that it almost guaranteed he would be stopped out, forcing him to take his money. The same attitude goes for the stop loss order. Nothing is as wasteful to a day trader as a market that wallows in a "no man's land" between small or no profit and small loss. Pat Arbor, the Chairman of the Board of Trade, tells a story in *The Outer Game of Trading* (Irwin, 1994) of Everett Clip, one of the senior members of the exchange.

> Everett will take a new trader and march him right down to the middle of the bond pit, and he'll say, "Now, watch this." And he'd say, "What's the market?" "Five bid at six sellers," someone says. Everett would say to the new trader, "Watch very closely." He then turns to the guy who gave him the market, "I'll sell you one at five and I'll buy one from you at six," Then he turns back to the young trader and says, "You see what I just did?" The young trader would kind of look, his eyes wide open and say, "Yeah, you just lost a tick." Everett then says triumphantly, "That's right. Never forget it!" You see, that's how you take a loss, dispassionately, no emotion. If you can learn that, you'll be a successful trader!

You're a day trader. Take that small loss. Move on with your business!

Taking profits, however, is another matter. A sound approach should include price or some other objective for the market's performance. A reasonable price objective will vary with the volatility and risk of each individual market. For example, many systems created for bonds reduce the risk to three to five ticks. Under those circumstances, trying to squeeze a basis point out of the market might be a little greedy. In other words, the reward should have some relationship to the risk taken. You also need to consider other objectives. How quickly does the market move in your favor after you enter? There's something to be said for instant gratification. Also, how does the market perform as it moves toward your price objective? Is it making a new high, then backing off, and then making another new high? Or did it go into a "fast" market condition but fall short of your price objective in the middle of the day? Reacting to these differences can add dollars to any system you are using.

Money Management

Many traders confuse risk management with money management. Risk management is what we have talked about above. It is taking small losses and managing the rewards in relation to the risks taken. Money management refers to the proper use of capital, and that includes using it for maximum benefit and preserving it for maximum longevity. It makes as little sense to commit, say, $100,000 to day trading and then trade one lot as it does to trade 100 lots. Arrive at a balance through careful consideration of your personal comfort level, risk parameters of each system and the volatility of the market being traded.

Keep in mind that short-term trading is like hitting singles and doubles and stealing bases to win baseball games. You can win a lot of games this way but only if you have a good defense.

Whatever method, approach or system you create for day or swing trading, you must resolve some important issues if you are to be successful. You must be able to view the market as a vehicle or tool from which your objective is to extract profits. Entering the market on your terms is your edge and reduces risk to the smallest possible level. However, as important as your entry into the market is, taking the money when it's available is a close second. Trying to turn a day or swing trade into a home run position dooms one to failure. Do not mix time frames. You cannot make a trade based on a five-minute chart and validate trying to turn that trade into a position. Your day trading goal is to enter the market with small risk, take your profit if given and move on to the next opportunity. Worrying about what you might be leaving on the table will distort your focus and inhibit you from making good decisions. *A sound approach or system will find more opportunity in the markets than you will be able to take advantage of.*

Another issue you must come to terms with is the sheer number of trades you will have to make as part of this process. Believe it or not, this is a real problem for many people. Whether it is because of the constant decision making, the flow of paper or a stream of losses, many people fold under the weight. And this goes for pit traders as well. A well-known clearing firm in Chicago assists traders on the floor of the exchange by teaching a proven method of scalping in the trading pit, that is, trading for the smallest of increments throughout the trading day. The first thing the trader is taught is to "scratch" or buy and sell at the same price. This serves to teach the trader to enter and exit the market quickly and to protect the trader if the market turns. But the most important aspect of this lesson is neither of these: The real lesson is to force the trader to make trades. Yes, to just make the trades! Even when the cost of a scratch is measured in pennies, many novice traders will spend a full trading day with less than a handful of trades on their trading cards. They have to be forced to enter and exit the market many times a day. I am not suggesting that an off-floor trader should or could trade for such small increments. However, the psychological barriers to making the trades are the same.

In the following pages I am going to show you my approach to day and swing trading. I say "approach" because I believe that the essential ingredients to a successful trading method are not the system but what qualities the trader brings to that system. By *approach* I mean the attitudes, emotions, focus and state of mind that the trader incorporates into whatever system or method he or she uses. My earliest training in trading was in classical chart analysis, and I really believe in keeping it simple. That is why, except for a few computer-generated numbers, which define the market's trend and create some support and resistance areas, my primary tool is the simple daily bar chart. Most of what you read here will apply in any time frame.

CHAPTER 5

The Innergame
Trading Approach

Keys to the Innergame Trading Approach

Some personal axioms integral to the Innergame Trading Approach are listed in Figure 5.1 and described thoroughly in this chapter.

Patience Is Your Edge

The edge for the floor trader is buying the bid and selling the offer, an unreasonable expectation for off-the-floor day traders. However, you can maintain an edge in other ways. Patience and preparation serve to create an edge that helps build and conserve equity. Knowing what you expect the market to do and waiting patiently for the market to come to you, to meet your expectations, gives you that edge.

FIGURE 5.1   Innergame Trading Approach Axioms

- Patience is your edge.
- Good day trades result from high percentage "setups."
- Anticipation of market opportunities is critical.
- Predetermined buy and sell areas must be executed.
- Trade one setup trade per market per day.
- Ignore the noise; follow the signal.
- Take "fast market" or climax condition profits.
- Avoid dull or nonperforming markets.

Good Day Trades Result from High Percentage "Setups"

You must view each day in a larger time frame, which might range from one day to two weeks of market action. Understanding how markets "set up" to make predictable moves and anticipating these moves through the setup are valuable keys to success.

Anticipation of Market Opportunities Is Critical

In most instances, waiting for the market to demonstrate what appears to be a trading opportunity results in entering too late for maximum profits.

Predetermined Buy and Sell Areas Must Be Executed

For those traders who have difficulty "pulling the trigger," putting resting orders in the market will get you into the trade.

Trade One Setup Trade Per Market Per Day

Overtrading comes from indecision and anxiety. By setting your sights on one good setup in a market, you avoid trading your emotions.

Ignore the Noise; Follow the Signal

Much of what a market does during the day can be considered *noise*, that is, market action without meaning. Hanging on every tick can be a wearisome and misdirected chore. You must eliminate your reactions to the noise and follow the essential signal.

Take "Fast Market" or Climax Condition Profits

In day or swing trading, it is a good idea to exit a profitable trade if the market climaxes on heavy tick volume or "fast market" conditions. It is a high probability that the high or low of the day is being made at this time. If the market hits your resting entry orders under these conditions, expect immediate profits or be alert for another wave in the same direction.

Avoid Dull or Nonperforming Markets

If you find yourself in a market that is very quiet, look elsewhere. Time is scarce, and watching a dull market will drain your energy.

Observe the Three Categories of Market Setups

The Innergame day and swing trading method is based on three categories of market setups: the market, the computer and the chart.

The Market Setup

The first setup stems from the natural rhythm of the market. In *The Taylor Trading Technique* (Traders Press), George Douglas Taylor describes it as a three- to five-day swing in the market. A swing low day that is followed by a sell day might mean an extension of the previous day and then a sell-short day that would then lead to the next buy day. Provision should be made for a strong or weak market that might extend the number of days in the swing to five. Figure 5.2 shows an example of this. Understanding where the market is in the swing helps to formulate a plan for any particular day.

The Computer Setup

For the Innergame Trading Method, I use just four proprietary computer-generated numbers. There is a short- and long-term trend identifier and a short- and long-term momentum oscillator. These are represented in Figure 5.3 by the dotted long-term trend number, the solid long-term pivot (derived from the LT oscillator), the short-term trend number line and the black dot short-term pivot.

This category can be any number of commonly used or esoteric computer-generated numbers that you, the trader, feel comfortable using. One common error, in my view, that many traders make is to rely on this tool to the exclusion of either the market setup or our next category, which I call *chart setup*.

The Chart Setup

Here I focus on using charting techniques that stand alone or are used in conjunction with our other setup categories. They include

1. Natural market retracements
2. Trendlines and pattern recognition

FIGURE 5.2 The Three-Day to Five-Day Swing

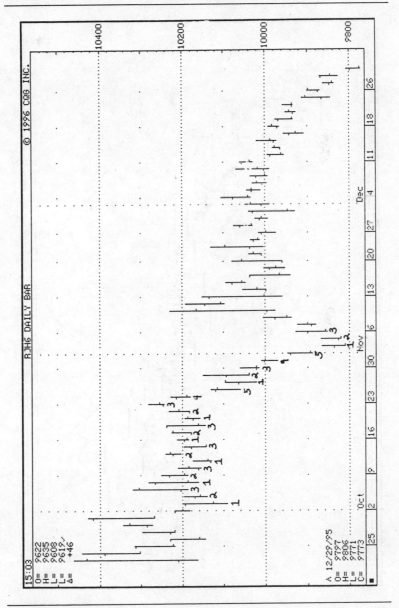

FIGURE 5.3 Trend Identifiers and Momentum Oscillators

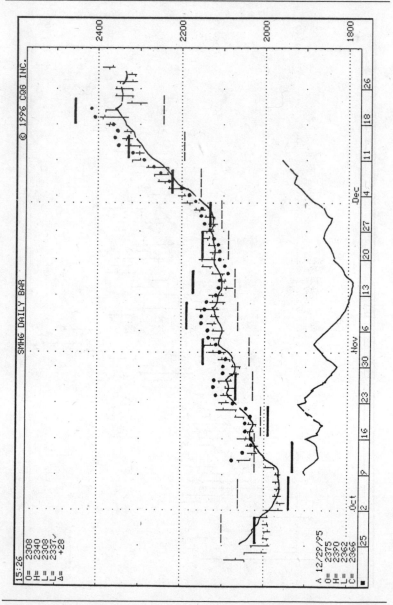

3. Daily or two-day patterns

4. Highs and lows

Natural market retracements. This technique includes Fibonacci ratios, Gann lines, Elliott Waves, etc. Figure 5.4 is an example of the S&P 500 finding resistance at the 50 percent retracement level. I also include in this category market retracements to moving averages. This setup is usually most effective when the market tests these areas on buy days or sell-short days in the natural swing.

Trendlines and pattern recognition. Many times the simplest devices are the most effective as we can see in Figure 5.5. The bottom triangle breakout gives the market support for four days with increasing volatility and opportunity. The simple trendline offers us three low-risk entry days, and the flags and pennant patterns are textbook. Traders may either buy the small pullbacks in the flag pattern or wait for the breakout and follow the market strength or weakness.

Daily or two-day patterns. These include at least five patterns (see Figure 5.6):

1. *Outside day* (OD) occurs when the day's range is above and below that of the previous day's range. The day following an outside day can usually be traded by buying dips and selling rallies.

2. *Inside day* (ID) occurs when the day's range is below the high and above the low of the previous day's range. Inside days are often followed by increased volatility and should be traded by buying the breakout above the previous day's high and selling a breakout below the previous day's low.

3. *Constricted range day* (CRD) occurs when the range contracts to the smallest range of the past several

FIGURE 5.4 Resistance at 50 Percent Retracement Level

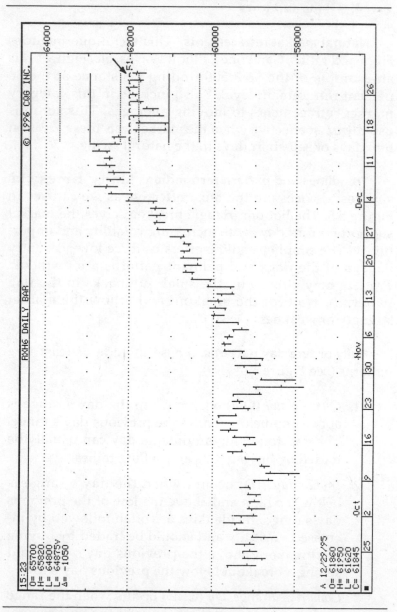

FIGURE 5.5 Simple but Revealing Trendlines and Patterns

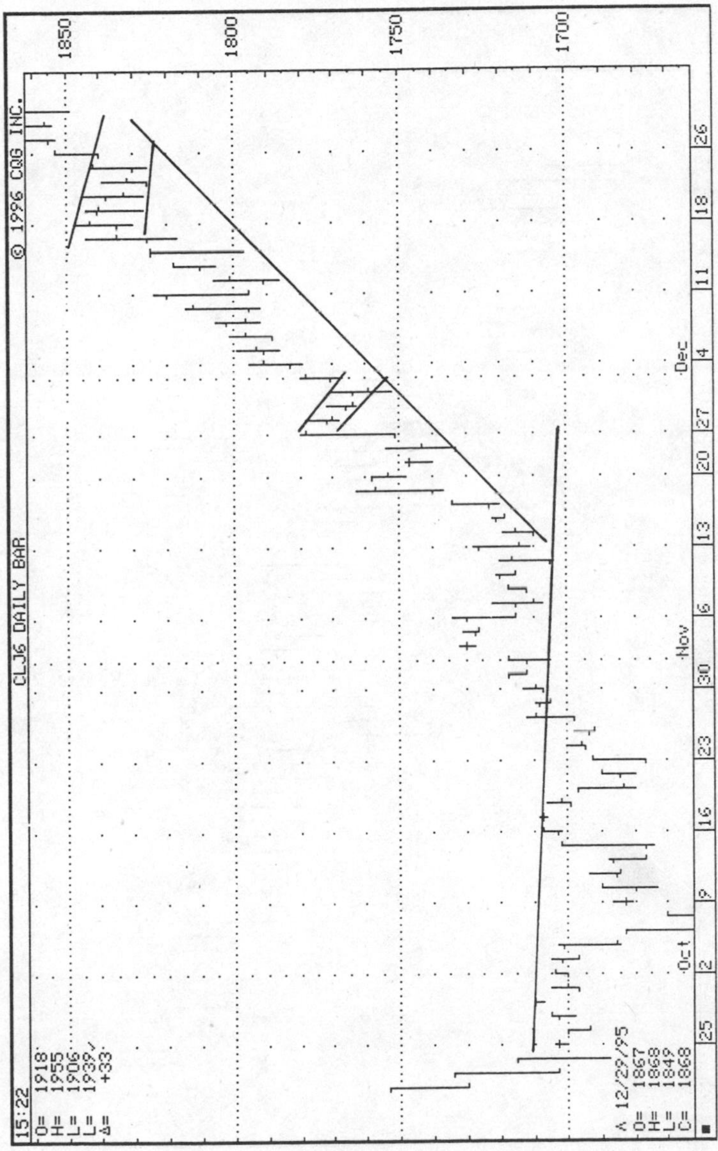

FIGURE 5.6 Daily or Two-Day Patterns

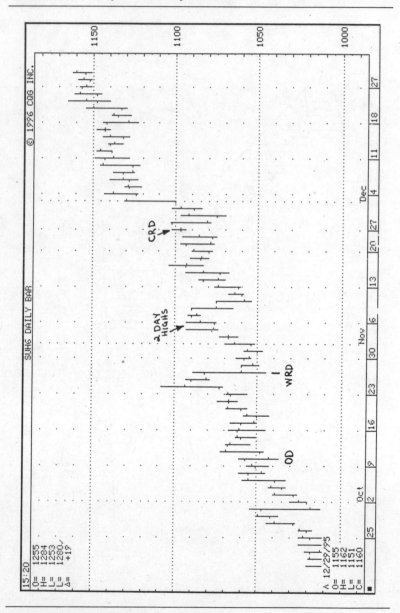

52

days. Sometimes the market will contract over two or more days. Patience here can provide opportunity. This is another pattern where the trader should be prepared to trade the breakouts in either direction.

4. *Wide range day* (WRD) is a range that is considerably larger than the past several days. Wide range days are usually followed by trading range days, and the trader should look to buy breaks and sell rallies.

5. *Two-day highs and lows* occur when markets tend to test the previous day's high or low and can provide the lowest risk trades available. When the trader can combine these tests with either a computer number setup or a chart setup, it becomes a very low-risk, potentially high reward trade.

Creating a Road Map for Trades

Consistency in planning is as important as consistency in execution. Preparation and planning in order to be able to anticipate market action can be effective only if traders are consistent with the various elements of their methodology.

The landmarks on the road map to a trade are listed in Figure 5.7 and are described below:

FIGURE 5.7   Landmarks on Trade Road Map

- Trend
- Swing location of the market
- Pattern recognition
- One- or two-day bar patterns
- Computer-generated numbers

Trend

The first landmark to identify is the market trend. My habit is to use simple daily bar charts with my computer-generated numbers superimposed onto the chart. Some traders are more number oriented and need merely to look at a set of numbers to fix the market in their minds. Although I enjoy modern technology, I have continued to update daily charts by hand because it reinforces a sense of continuity for each market even though there may not have been any trade opportunities. The important point is that the trader determines in his or her mind if this market is in an up trend, down trend or sideways trend. Simple trendlines or higher highs and higher lows and lower highs and lower lows will establish a trend. I have also included my proprietary computer-generated numbers on my charts because they have a strong reliability for anticipating support and resistance areas of the market. As you can see in Figure 5.8, the corn market was well into an uptrend when it retraced and traded on the long-term trend ID area. This creates low-risk opportunities for day and swing traders. The operative word here is *low*, not *no* risk. Traders who are looking for the no-risk trade will forever be complaining about the markets that "got away."

Many traders use the Innergame Trading Portfolio fax service as a guide to the important support and resistance areas in up to 20 markets.

Another example of the use of trend identification is shown in Figure 5.9. This soybean chart shows an uptrend and Fibonacci retracement numbers superimposed onto it. As you can see, anticipating a retracement test of either .384 or .50 of the October-November uptrend put traders in position to make very low-risk trades with large potential. In later sections we will see how swing analysis and daily bar patterns help to trade this market on a day-trade and swing-trade basis. However, notice how the market could not make it to the full .50 correction and then found support on subsequent days both at previous days' lows

FIGURE 5.8 Identifying Market Trends

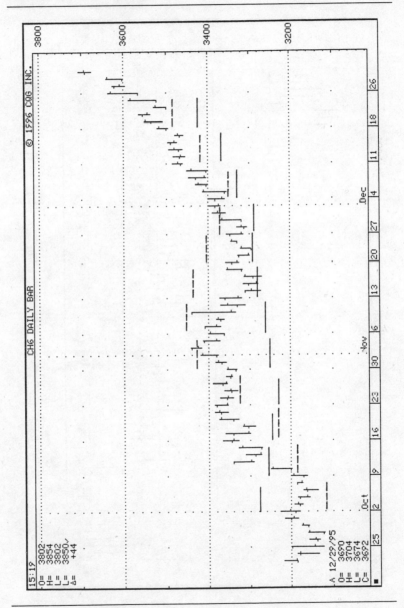

FIGURE 5.9 Low-Risk Entry in an Uptrend

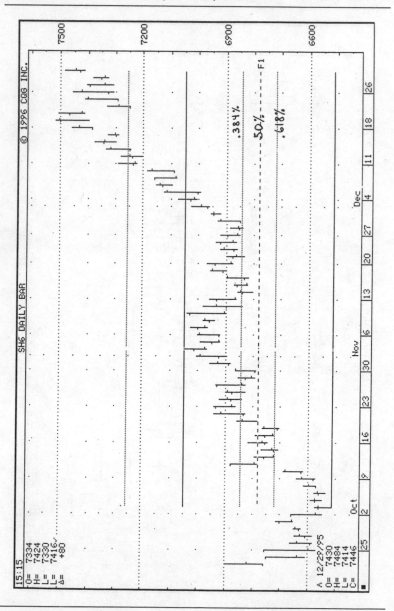

and the .384 Fibonacci price level. Realistically, no one can know whether this market goes up or down from this correction point. But we have found a high probability setup, and that is all one can ask for. The point here is not the specific method shown in this section on trend identification; it is that whatever method you feel comfortable using should be the first thing on your daily agenda.

Swing Location of the Market

Determining where a market is in its three- to five-day swing pattern will improve profitability. In *The Taylor Trading Technique*, the author breaks the market down to a buy day, a sell day and a sell-short day. Once this rhythm is established, the trader should also pay attention to how and when the lows and highs are made each day. For example, buy days should have lows made first, and sell-short days should have highs made first. For the most part, experienced traders have always sensed that morning lows in a market are a low-risk buy area. The old adage of buying a lower opening in a bull and selling a higher opening in a bear is still a viable operating procedure. And it is also a very important rule for day traders as well.

Morning weakness into support has a good potential to react profitably as the day wears on. However, most afternoon breaks into support are not as reliable. The same, of course, goes for morning strength into resistance. So as day and swing traders, we should be aware of the swing location setup as well as the daily setup in order to maximize our profit potential. Let's follow this on our old friend the soybean market. (See Figure 5.10.) I have labeled the swing high with an S, and then I counted two days for a possible buy day. The second day, labeled B, met our expectation of a buy day. After a weak close in the previous day, the market opened lower and made its lows first as it proceeded to rally for the rest of the day, closing near its highs. In such a situation, day traders are content; swing traders will sell the higher opening that does take place on the fol-

FIGURE 5.10 Find the Swing Location of the Market

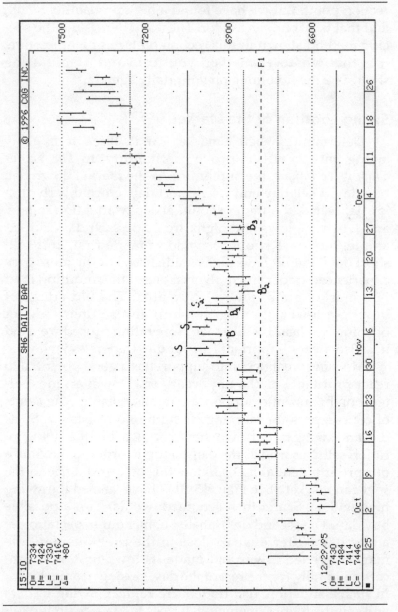

lowing day (S1). The next day was a constricted range day (CRD) and would be a sell-short day as well. CRDs, which we will talk about later, will often signal increased volatility and wider ranges. This occurred the next day, labeled B1. This would be a buy day possibility except that the market opened sharply higher, essentially testing the swing high of the move, and proceeded to break all day into the close. The rule is this: Don't buy a weak close even on a buy day because the probability for a lower opening is very good. As it turns out, we got a steady opening and a break into the Fibonacci .384 retracement area. The market found its support and rallied for the remainder of the day. The next day (S2) is a sell day, and after the highs are made early, the market closes on its lows, setting up a lower opening and a test of the Fibonacci .50 retracement area, B2. As we moved several days to the bar marked B3, we saw that this potential buy day turned into a constricted range day still sitting on the support area. The next day turned into the anticipated buy day with a low made on the opening and a strong market through the close. As I mentioned earlier, Taylor describes a three- to five-day swing pattern, and this is an example of being able to be on the alert for a buying opportunity one day removed.

Pattern Recognition

Sometimes the most important landmarks are based on the simplest concepts. Trendlines that define several days of highs or lows create tests that are low-risk opportunities. (See Figure 5.11.) The buy-day bar, B, was followed by a sell-day rally to the trendline, and the next day, a sell-short day, never violated that trendline. There were two other subsequent tests of this same trendline. In Figure 5.12, we see an example of a triangle pattern and the breakout out of that pattern for a day or swing trade. You can see that the triangle formation ends with three constricted range days in a row setting up the volatile move. Although breakout moves, or gap openings, are difficult to enter, they often

FIGURE 5.11   Sell Day Rally into Trendline

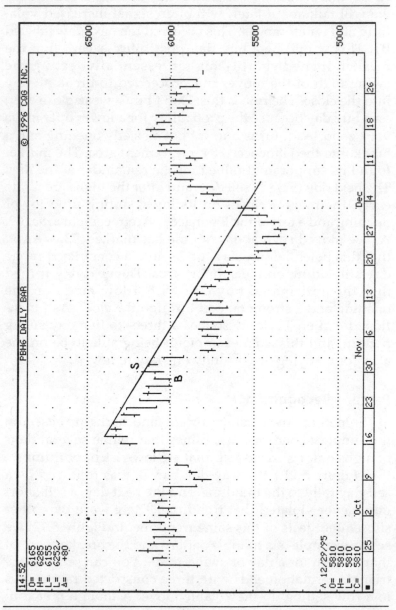

FIGURE 5.12 Breakout from a Triangle Pattern

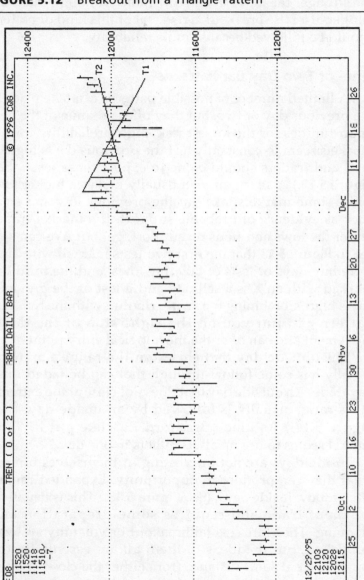

© Copyright 1996 CQG INC.

yield large payoffs. Many times the wider the gap opening, the stronger the move in that direction. Although there is a danger of a false breakout, a reversal of this kind of pattern should be followed because of its reliability.

One- or Two-Day Bar Patterns

A limited number of possible patterns can take place in the previous day or two, but they offer us some of the best opportunities for the lowest risk, high probability trades. Markets seem to constantly test the previous day's high or low, and traders should come to expect these tests. (See Figure 5.13.) A strong market usually makes a higher low, while some markets take out the previous low and snap back as evidence of probable support. If a market trades under the lows and finds no support, get out. We can also see in Figure 5.13 that the first two tests marked with an X were buy days or tests of buy day lows, and the third bar marked with an X is a sell day and a test of the previous day's high. Combining the swing rhythm with the two-day pattern can put you on the right side of the day's movement and can offer the most logical entry point.

The outside day that closes on the range's extreme usually has some follow-through that can be faded for a day trade. An outside day that does not close at the extreme of its range usually is followed by an inside day. (See Figure 5.14.) As Linda Bradford Raschke put it, "The market seems to use up all its bullets in one day."

Inside days are not interesting in themselves but for what they can produce in opportunity. Expanded ranges often follow inside days. (See Figure 5.15.) This is usually a breakout trade and requires some preparation and planning. There are several breakout or volatility systems published, but the ideas in them all are essentially the same. Enter at some distance from either the close or open or high or low of the previous bar or of the second previous bar. I believe the high and low of the previous day work well, and, if there is a failure of the move, give the trader the opportunity to turn around on the trade with a reasonable risk parameter.

Constricted range days—either one or several in a row—also portend expanded ranges and breakout trades. The extent of the constriction is relative to the ranges over several recent days. (See Figure 5.16.) The same methodology for breakout trades used above for the inside day can be used for constricted range days. There are more occurrences of whipsaw action, but the narrow ranges keep the losses so circumscribed that turning on the trade and going the opposite way is a sound trading tactic.

I've mentioned expanded ranges several times, and as traders it is nice to be on the right side of them. However, we have seen that being aware of them offers opportunities on subsequent days. So I include them as an important category.

Computer-Generated Numbers

There are no magic numbers. And certainly no magic numbers that can stand alone as a full trading system. Numbers are a tool just as all the elements we have already discussed are tools to be used together. I use three types of computer-generated numbers that are calculated for two different time frames. The trend identifiers I mark in dotted lines and the long line, an oscillator at the bottom or top of the chart and the pivots in solid, short lines and dots which are derived from the oscillator. (See Figure 5.17.)

The pivot numbers are the prices the market must continue to exceed in order to maintain the current slope of the oscillator. When the pivot moves from above to below the market or vice versa, the market's range tends to expand and should be traded in that direction. The pivots also are reliable price points for support and resistance on a daily basis.

As a market's trend flattens out, it will trade between the intermediate-term trend price and the intermediate-term pivot. This will define the sideways trend that develops either as a continuation pattern, a bottom, or a top.

(See Figure 5.18.) While this is taking place, the short-term pivot and either of the intermediate-term prices become support and resistance areas and many times define the day's ranges. (See Figure 5.19.)

The short-term oscillator represented by the line graph on the bottom of Figure 5.20 is a very useful tool. It has definite overbought and oversold areas that allow us at Innergame to take advantage of the pivot movement and either exit a current position or take a new one at or near the tops and bottoms of market swings. The oscillator also sets up divergence, another useful tool.

Many useful computer-generated systems are available—ADX, MACD, Stochastics, RSI, Bollinger Bands, etc. However, it is a mistake to isolate these devices and trade only on their input. Each trader must find the most comfortable tools and blend them into a methodology that fits his or her personality. The computer numbers of the Innergame Trading Approach have been traded day in and day out for over 15 years. During this time they have been refined, tested and retested to assure their reliability in different market conditions. That is where my market confidence comes from. Having said all this, I still realize it is only a number!

Moving from One Winning Trade to Another

We have discussed all the landmarks on the road map to trading success, but we cannot reach our destination if we don't plan our trip and hit the gas pedal. No serious traveler goes on a journey without taking out a map and thinking through the various alternatives, obstacles and scenarios that the trip might entail. It is the same with trading!

Hundreds of interviews, close personal relationships with some of the country's best traders and my personal market experiences have taught me this: I have not met a consistently profitable trader who hasn't prepared rigorously for trading. The most important part of your preparation must be preparing yourself emotionally, psychologically and physically to be resourceful, disciplined and committed to whatever the market throws your way.

Remember, it all comes down to these three things:

1. Identifying an opportunity

2. Taking action automatically

3. Feeling good about the trade

Identifying an Opportunity

It's decision time. You have all these tools to identify one or more opportunities based on probability. You have found the swing location, or a double bottom or top setup, an inside day setup for a possible breakout. Write them down and be prepared to act!

Taking Action Automatically

You must be resolved, disciplined and consistent in acting upon your ideas and hard work. Every day that the market behaves as you have anticipated will reinforce your discipline and feelings of trading confidence.

Feeling Good about the Trade

Each trade you have made following this format is a good trade whether it turns a profit or a loss. Trading is a process, and the result at the end of the process is the important thing, not each small element (individual trade) of that process. Your small losses are just operating costs that you have made to generate business. You must truly believe this and operate from this market attitude. The Innergame Trading Approach is based on this precept.

FIGURE 5.13   Tests of Previous Day's Highs and Lows

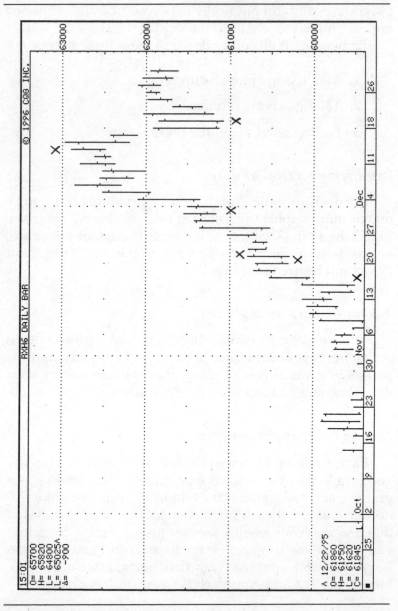

FIGURE 5.14 Outside Days

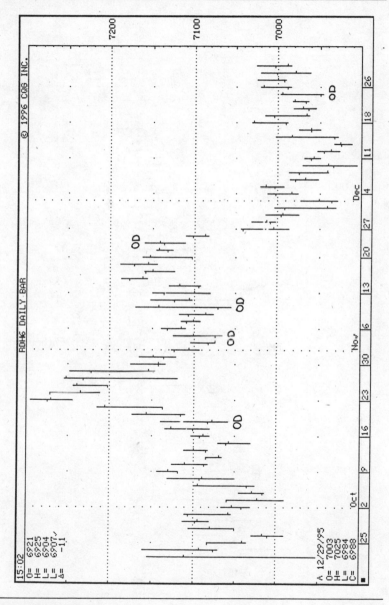

FIGURE 5.15 Inside Days

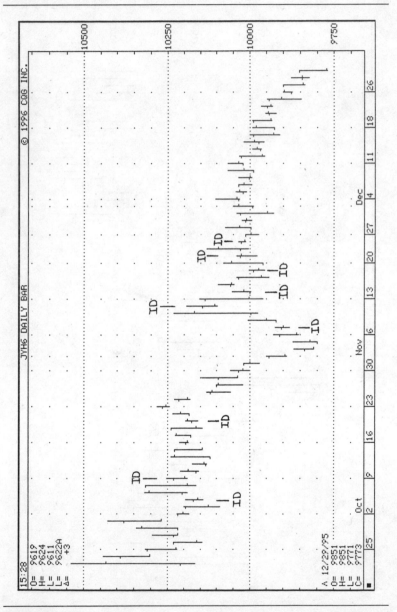

FIGURE 5.16 Constricted Range Days

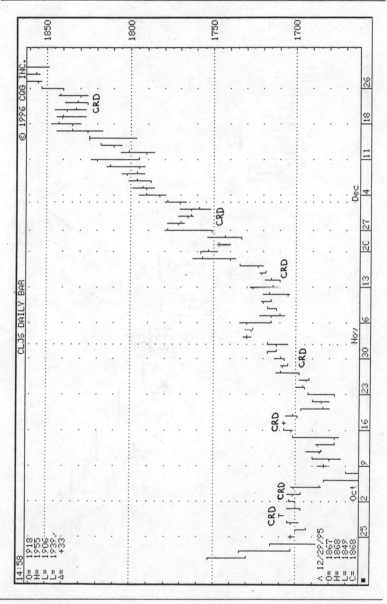

FIGURE 5.17 Computer-Generated Numbers

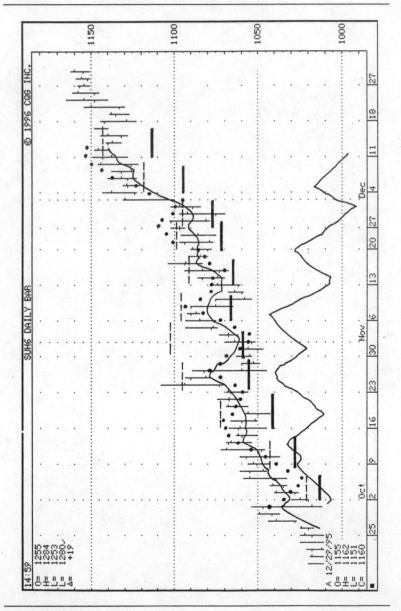

FIGURE 5.18 Flattening Market Trend

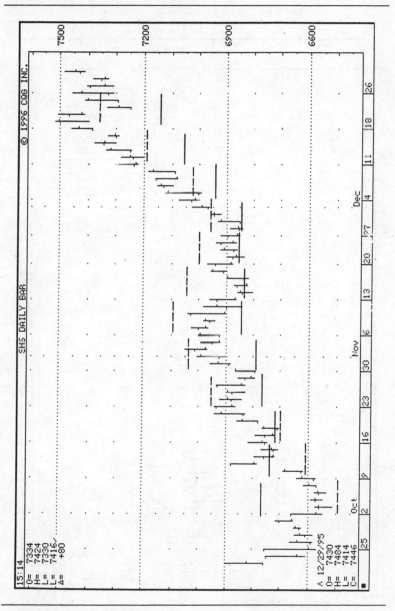

FIGURE 5.19 Support and Resistance Between Intermediate and Daily Points

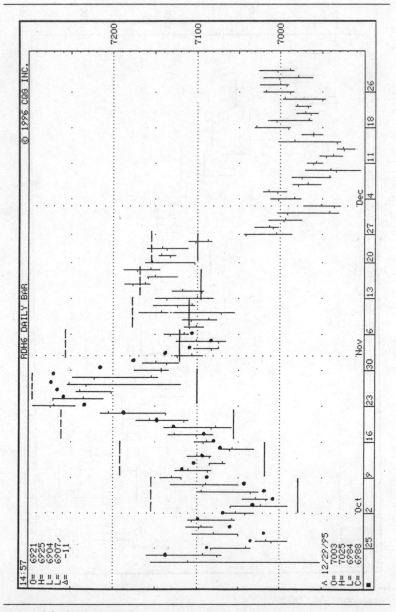

FIGURE 5.20 The Useful Short-Term Oscillator

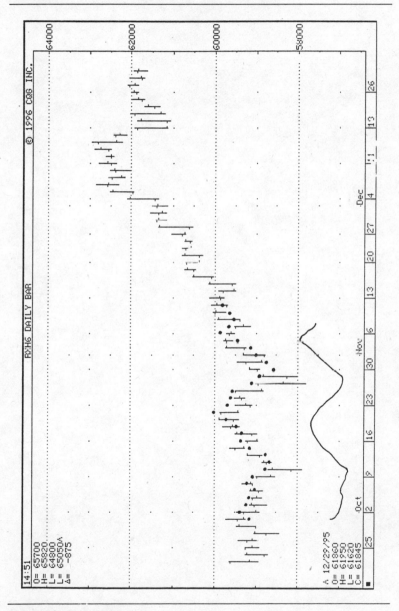

PART THREE

Expert Perspectives on Day Trading

CHAPTER 6

Bill Williams

Bill Williams, Ph.D. is the founder of the Profitunity Trading Group and has been actively trading for over 35 years. His innovative work into the physics of conscious ness produced a new way of looking at psychotherapy and the interaction between the trader's psyche and the market. Dr. Williams is the developer of the Market Facilitation Index (MFI), now standard on many analytical computer programs worldwide, and he is the discoverer of the fractal of the Elliott Wave. Dr. Williams is recognized as the fore-most active trader using fractals and the science of chaos. He is the author of the recently published book, *Trading Chaos: Applying Expert Techniques to Maximize Profits* (Wiley, 1995).

Q: *How long did it take you to come up with a successful day trading approach?*

Bill: I kid you not, almost 30 years! Actually, I really didn't start to day trade seriously until 1980. Up until that time, from about 1959 to 1980, I was mainly a position trader, trading both stocks and futures. In 1980, I began trading just futures. I haven't traded or owned a stock since then, and I don't ever plan to.

Q: *So how long did it take you to come up with the approach that you are using now?*

Bill: Really, it was a gradual process, a sort of metamorphosis. I don't trade at all today like I did 15 years ago. I have been trading exactly as I trade now for about four years. So to answer your question precisely, my particular approach to day trading developed over an 11-year period, and most of the improvements had to do specifically with the research we were doing in the science of chaos and nonlinear dynamics.

Q: *Was this research computer-based or perceptual in terms of what you were expressing in the market?*

Bill: It started off as computer-based. It included research in nonlinear feedback calculus, which is very complex mathematically; it really takes a mainframe computer. After the mainframe had completed the mathematical process, then we spent about three years turning those mathematical findings into a pattern recognition system.

Q: *Which is what you use now, right?*

Bill: Yes. What we use now is based on the science of chaos, as opposed to what's normally thought of as traditional technical analysis. And what we do is look at the market from five different dimensions. We believe from our research that the market is at least a five-dimensional animal. Price and time are two dimensions, but we think at least three other dimensions need to be considered.

Q: *What were some of your early attempts at day trading like?*

Bill: If you remember, in the early '80s, it was the heyday of the black box trading systems and the mechanical systems. I went through a number of those systems at great expense, not only for the actual expense of the systems, but I paid dearly for the failure of the systems. After that experience I became disillusioned with mechanical trading systems. I should add here that, although all of our indicators are completely unambivalent, our approach is not a mechanical one. But to return to your question, I became disillusioned with these systems and traditional technical analysis as well. I felt many of these systems were based on a false assumption, that the future is going to be like the past.

I see the market as an ever-unfolding phenomenon. It is something that is constantly changing. So my approach to trading is an unfolding behavioral approach as opposed to a traditional technical analytical one that looks for some pattern in the past and then tries to identify a market where that pattern will replicate itself.

Q: *But, Bill, your system is a pattern recognition system.*
Bill: Yes. Absolutely.

Q: *So are you looking for new patterns? Is that what you're saying, or are you reacting to familiar patterns in a whole new way?*
Bill: Well, let me break it down like this. We're trying to see the market in a whole new way. Traditional physics looks at space, time, mass and energy, and we think the market contains the same things. We look at space through the lens of the fractal; we deal with time through our interpretation of the area wave. The mass is obviously volume. I'm a long-time student of volume. And then the energy is the momentum.

We look at the market's energy in two different phases. We look at the momentum itself, and then we look very closely at what we call the acceleration/deceleration or the change in momentum.

Our theory is based on our hypothesis that prices don't really create any kind of causative factor in the market. What changes before price is momentum, and what changes before momentum is volume, and what changes before volume is all the crazy traders in the world making these crazy decisions. So our best trading, our best entries, are always based on momentum as opposed to price change.

You see it's a whole new look at the market—the old assumptions don't work! Black box systems were based again on a false assumption. What happened is that when computers became affordable and practical for people to own, it became easy to program a computer so that it would take past data and figure out an ideal system. But the more ideal that system is and the more profitable it proves to be in the past, the more it is an absolute guarantee that it's not going to work in the future, because for it to work in the future, the future has to be an exact repetition of the past!

As I said before, I tried a number of these black box systems. In fact, I was into it so much that I created several dozen of them myself, but none of them really worked. Some of them would work for a very short time, but basically all of them died in the end. And as evidence of that, look at the hundreds of different black box systems back in the early '80s selling then for $3,000 or more that to my knowledge are not around anymore. Not a single one of them is in use today.

Q: *Bill, based on your many years of experience, what do you feel is the key to a really successful day trading system?*

Bill: I think the key is that you have to look at the underlying structure of the market as opposed to looking at the indicators of the market. For example, the most obvious indicator that's around, I guess, is a breakout; you know, when the market goes through its trading range or a congestion area. The only problem with a breakout is that if you buy a breakout, you get the world's worst trade location. You end up buying the highs and the lows. There's nothing instinctively wrong with that, except you don't have an edge. So here's what we try to do—our goal in day trading is twofold: (1) We want to take 90 percent of any trend out, which is to say we want to buy on the bottom 10 percent or we want to sell on the top 10 percent; and (2) we buy and sell on all five dimensions. What that allows us to do on a very consistent basis is take three to five times the amount of the trend out of the market. So if the S&P has a trend run during the day of 500 points, we're really looking for 1,500 to 2,500 points out of that 500-point move.

Q: *Why do you think so many people think it's impossible to day trade successfully?*

Bill: Well, I know that there are people in this industry, some very, very good traders that I respect a great deal, who say that a person is absolutely crazy, *loco*, to even think of day trading. I think one of the problems, particularly when you're day trading, is that you have to deal with a fast market. Consequently you have to have something that moves, such as the currencies or the S&P. For most inexperienced traders these are very scary markets. The S&P market can move, as you know, hundreds of points in a couple of minutes. I think that what happens is that fear takes over. And whenever a trader is trading from fear, we are absolutely, from a psychological standpoint, going to be the most consistent traders ever. The only problem is that we buy the tops and sell the bottoms. We do exactly the wrong thing when we're coming from a fearful state of mind. And since the S&P is a fearful market, a powerful market, because it can change so fast and go so far, a lot of people I think are just simply petrified.

Q: *Speaking of state of mind, what do you think is the optimum psychology for successful day trading?*

Bill: I think the psychology is more important than the methodology. I think your attitude is more important than your aptitude in trading. I think most people are just very afraid of the market. One of the things we always ask people who come to our tutorial is: What kind of animal is the market? And invariably they will say, particularly with respect to the S&P, it's a gorilla or a snake or something that's very threatening. One of our goals, and one of my personal goals, is to be friends with the market and not get mad at the market, because the market truly is a very neutral thing. And one of the ways that we look at our trading from a psychological standpoint is to determine to what extent we can say, "I don't care which way the market goes." When I truly don't care, I know I'm trading properly because I'm in tune with the market. But if I'm sitting there saying, "I hope it goes up, I hope it goes up, I hope it goes up," then I know I'm in trouble, because I'm trying to manipulate the market. I think the secret of trading any market is to give up your own personality and your own wishes. You have to concentrate on being one with the market. It's almost a Zen-like thing.

Q: *Zen-like?*

Bill: Zen-like. I also think that good trading is almost like a religion in the sense that you're giving up your personality to a larger, greater force, and that larger, greater force is the market. So I think there's a lot of parallels between good trading and religion!

Q: *In your opinion, what would be the optimum trading psychology for day trading?*

Bill: Well, I think the optimal psychology is that you don't think about the dollars. You don't think about the number of points you are up or down. I think at the end of a day of day trading an inappropriate question is, "How much money did I make or lose today?" I think the only appropriate question is, "How in tune was I with the market?" And there will be days when you will be absolutely in tune with the market and you still will lose money. There will also, of course, be a lot of days when, if you're in tune with the market, you'll make much more money than you ever dreamed possible. I think you can be out of tune and make money but not on a consistent basis.

So our whole approach is to be at one with the market. For example, I think one of the best books on day trading there is doesn't say anything about day trading. It's a book by Alan Watts. He was a philosopher who wrote a book about Zen called *The Wisdom of Insecurity*. I think it's a great book for a day trader. It doesn't say anything about trading, no systems or anything of that sort, but one of the illustrations he uses in the introduction of the book, for example, is that if you fall in the water, and you're fearful of the water and start fighting the water, you're probably going to drown. But if you fall in the water, and you just relax and float, the very thing that you're afraid of will keep you afloat and save your life. I think that's a very good analogy to the market.

Q: *Are you trying to say that most day traders go into the markets and are ready to sink?*

Bill: Oh yes, I definitely think so. I think most day traders, at least the day traders I have been associated with, by and large, are very fearful. When they go into a trade, you can actually see them physically tense up. I mean, their shoulders will start to slump and their head will go forward, and they tighten up. And I think that's very, very bad, both psychologically and physiologically. I think it's a great hindrance.

Q: *I have found that people who are tense tend not to be capable of hearing or seeing what the market is offering them.*

Bill: Well, I think you're exactly right, and I think there's some physiological basis for this. For example, when you get tense, you normally cut off most of the oxygen to your brain, so you really can't think as well. You think much better, much more rationally, when you're not tense. When you're tense, you tend to react, and reacting fearfully in the market oftentimes is fatal.

Q: *Could you speak more about your trading methodology?*

Bill: Well, basically, since we're trying to get in tune with the market, it is trend following, but not trend following on the traditional breakout mode. I can tell you what we're looking for, by way of an illustration. If you were to roll a bowling ball down the street, the momentum of that bowling ball will keep it going until it either stops by friction or it starts rolling up an incline and slows to a halt. Now, the market will do the same thing. The market will keep its current momentum until some new information comes along. One of the definitions of chaos is new information. According to this idea, chaos or new information moves the market. But now going back to the bowling ball, if it is rolling down the street and it hits an incline, the ball will roll up that incline until it loses its momentum, turns around and then rolls back down the hill. That turning around and rolling back down the hill is like the market changing trend. When that bowling ball starts to slow down, from a physics standpoint, it's really accelerating in the opposite direction. Our first entry is on what we call the acceleration/deceleration index or the AC/DC Index, and that measures the change in momentum. So as soon as that momentum starts to change—and momentum will always change before price does—we have a signal for entry. That's what allows us to get in on the bottom 10 percent and out on the top 10 percent. Then, when that momentum turns around, when that bowling ball loses its momentum and turns back the other way, we're already in the market. So we get on and repeat this process on every indication that the market tells us to add on. So we add on very rapidly.

Now, in the S&P, you are really only in a trend about 15 percent to 30 percent of the time. The rest of the time you're in a sideways market. Consequently, when you're in a trend, you have to be very, very aggressive. So we add on to our position on all five dimensions. Anytime we get a signal on any one of the five dimensions—to go long for example—we'll add on. We get out of all of our longs on the first negative signal from any one of the five dimensions. Then when we're in a bracketed market, which happens the majority of the time, we tend to make a little bit of money or tread water. But most of the money we make is in the trend.

Q: *In those bracketed markets, you tend to get signals to go either way, but your stops are very close to where you enter, aren't they?*
Bill: They're very close.

Q: *Are you moving from different time frames for your analysis when you're day trading?*
Bill: Yes.

Q: *Do you go from a daily to a 60, or to how short a time frame will you go?*
Bill: Well, what I like to do, particularly in the S&P— and we've done years and years of research on this—we like to trade down to the five-minute, and we like to trade the five-minute as long as it has 20 ticks per five-minute bar. If the volume goes down below 20 ticks per five-minute bar, what we'll normally do is just switch up and trade a 10-minute chart.

Q: *Right. So you're moving from time frame to time frame based on certain technical criteria that you've set up.*
Bill: Yes, based on volume. Now if we expect to be in a sideways market all day and we want to trade that day, what we'll do is go down to a three-minute chart.

Q: *How did you arrive at your current methodology?*
Bill: Well, I'll tell you, I was not trading successfully. I had been trading since 1959. Then in 1980 I decided to trade full-time, and when I did that, my profits dropped off. I

had subscribed to all kinds of newsletters. I was tapping all sorts of night lines, and none of that was helping. I decided to throw everything away and simply go with what the market was telling me. About that time a guy by the name of Benoit did some research at the IBM Research Center at Yorktown, New York, where he found that the fractal number, which is a measure of irregularity of the Mississippi River, was the same as the cotton and corn price. And learning that information changed my whole trading career. It indicated to me that the markets are a very natural process. They're not economic. They're not fundamental, not technical, nor are they mechanical; they're a natural function. From his point of view the markets are like the weather, and you may be able to be very accurate in foretelling what the weather is going to be in the next 15 minutes, but it's much more difficult to forecast what it's going to be next week. So the principle of chaos that we trade is how the market is unfolding right now, immediately, as opposed to projecting and saying, "Well, we're at this point, and next week we're going to be at that point." We just trade what's coming off the chart right now!

Q: *How do you deal with the losses that you have to sustain as a natural part of the process?*

Bill: Well, I think that is right; it is a natural part of the process. I think this is generally true with traders and has certainly been true with me. I have always learned a great deal more from my losses than from my profits. When I have a very good winner, I think I'm pretty smart, but when I have losses, I tend to study and try to figure out what happened and see if I can keep it from happening again. I think, as I said before, it's imperative to view the market as your friend. And I know that when I lose, it's because I'm out of tune with the market. You hear a lot of people blaming the market, and even professional traders say things that are totally inaccurate, such as "The market stopped me out." The market has never stopped anybody out! You get stopped out because you've made a decision, and that decision to get stopped out may have been in tune with the market or it may not have been. It may just be another case of trading in a state of fear. My whole emphasis is that I am committed, totally committed, that if I can give up my own personal bias and just be an obedient servant to the market and do what the market is telling me to do right now on the five dimensions I have mentioned, then the market will take great care of me!

Q: *Do you say anything to yourself in terms of the losses when they occur?*

Bill: Not really. You know, I grew up with older traders saying things like, "You should love your losses," and this sort of thing, and that never really made a lot of sense to me. But I do obviously think losses are a part of it. But with our trading technique, using these five dimensions, we're getting long or short on all of them all the time. If we're going in a direction, we will go in the other direction on the first signal that goes the other way. Doing that cuts down our amount of loss so it is very small. We just rarely experience a large loss per contract.

Q: *But in the bracketed markets, in that time period when you might have two or three days that the market is congesting and you're constantly taking very small losses, they do add up. How do you deal with it then?*

Bill: Well, I deal with it by realizing that the biggest moves always come from dull markets, from bracketed markets. So when we're in a bracketed market, and it's looking very dull, that's when we have to be the sharpest, because that's where the opportunities are developing. And what we get paid for, as traders, is seeing a change in the market or a change in the paradigm of the market before other people do. Once it comes out in *The Wall Street Journal* or on FNN, it's too late to get in!

We have our own indicator, which we call a *balance line*, that is the exact point where the attraction of two different strange attractors—that's chaos talk—takes place. But we have a point where it turns into the "Continental Divide." If the market is above that point, the market is going to go up; if it's below that point, the market is going to go down. Now, that point or that line will always go through the market in a dull market. I mean, the high and low will go on each side of it, so when it pulls away from that line, then we get very interested in going in that direction. So to answer your question, we don't really have any fear of bracketed markets, which doesn't mean we don't take losses. But we know that if we can sort of tread water during those times, the losses will be very small, and, at the other times, we will be very profitable, provided of course we get in the trend.

Now, most traders that I know generally take only about 20 percent to 30 percent out of a trend, and we're trying to get in to take out 80 percent. And we do it! The only way we can do it is by being in the market before it is obvious to other people.

Q: *It seems to me that one of the unique aspects of your system is that when the market starts to roll your way, you're adding contracts all the time, which for some people is kind of an uncomfortable thing to do. Of course, for you it's maximizing the market that's developing at that moment.*

Bill: Absolutely.

Q: *Okay. We've spoken of losses, but how do you deal with the profits?*

Bill: Basically, I don't worry about the profits. I never calculate how much a position has in dollars. I only look at the market in terms of the market telling me to go the other way. So if the market goes up and then comes back down and takes a sizable amount of my profit out, I will not reverse or I will not get out until the market tells me to. I don't make that decision; I let the market tell me to do that.

Q: *I know you mentioned this before, but are you telling me you don't think about the equity that you're giving up at all?*

Bill: I really don't. I think that I learned this early in my career. I happened to get the chance to trade with a 92-year-old trader, who was sharp as a tack. He was a tall, slender guy, and he called me Little Willy. I had been trading with him not very long at all, maybe an hour, when he looked over at me and said, "Little Willy, if you breathed like you trade, you'd be dead in five minutes." I said, "What are you talking about?" And he said, "Well, all you want to do is suck air." I said, "I still don't know what you're talking about." And he said, "Well, trading is like breathing. You inhale, and you take in enough oxygen that you need and maybe a little extra, and then you exhale and let somebody else have the rest of that oxygen. All you want to do is take every penny of your profits, and if you breathed like that, all you would be doing is inhaling and you'd be dead in five minutes." And I have never forgotten that lesson.

Q: *Well, you do know that there are many successful traders whose trading philosophy is, "If I have a profit, I'm not going to let it get away." You know that they're willing to just exit the market as quickly as they possibly can to pocket it and ring the register.*

Bill: Well, all I can say is that does not work for me. I know that there are a lot of things that other traders do, and there are a lot of people who say that you should never turn a profit into a loss and that good money management is never losing more than X amount of dollars. For example, I know some S&P day traders who say they will never take over a 100 point or a $500 loss. From my point of view, that's stupid trading, because you're trading your wallet, and you're not trading the market. My wallet will not help me trade the market profitably. I know that! The only way I can be profitable—and this may not work for everybody—is to be so in tune with the market that I'm going to do what the market tells me and try not to dictate to it by listening to my wallet.

Q: *Why do you think that people are unable to day trade successfully?*

Bill: I think part of it is this whole notion of risk-free trading. We're brought up, and you and I have talked about this before, with the sage advice of our parents not to take risks. We're inundated with that when we're children, and here we are in a profession of taking risk on purpose. So people figure the risk/reward ratio, the projected target, the projected profits, all of this sort of thing, and actually they should be out there seeking risk; in fact, seeking risks that other people are not taking. That's not the attitude of most day traders. Most day traders, as I've already mentioned, approach the market with a great deal of fear and intimidation.

Q: *Bill, you run tutorials year round. You have a lot of successful students. What is the psychological baggage many of these students bring with them that makes it difficult for them to be successful?*

Bill: I think that's the $64,000 question. I think there are two key things—one of them is that most people who go into commodity trading have already been successful, or at least most of the people who come to study with us are successful people. Most of them are professional people. They are or have been successful in business. We know from actual research that as a group commodity traders are in the top 10 percent of intelligence of the whole country. So you've got successful people, intelligent people, who come to day trading and 90 percent of them are not successful in it.

I think the problem is that the things that make you successful in other areas do not contribute to your success in trading. The second key factor is this ability to give up your own ego. Our basic belief, our fundamental belief, is that nobody trades the market; we all trade our belief system, and another word for our belief system is our ego. So we're all ego traders, and if we're going to get in tune with the market, the big issue is to give up our egos. So I think good trading is much more a psychological problem than it is methodological.

When you get right down to it, there are really only two ways to fail at day trading: inaccurate analysis or inappropriate implementation of an accurate analysis. So the first step is that you have to understand the underlying structure of the market, and we're not talking about the facade of prices. We're not talking about the price chart, because that's not the cause, that's the effect, and that's what most people unfortunately pay most attention to. The second thing I think that you have to have is understanding of your own personal underlying structure because most of us don't have enough money to move the market. What we have to do is change our own underlying structure to fit the market. Then, if we can align our own personal underlying structure to that of the market, then winning should become the path of least resistance. It should just be floating down the river. Our trading becomes very low stress. In our trading room we don't get real excited. We normally sit here with the cat and the dog in the room with classical music on. It's not a hectic place at all. The atmosphere is almost meditative.

So the two keys, again, are understanding the market—how it works, the underlying structure, momentum and from our standpoint, the five dimensions of the market—and the second and equally, if not more, important thing is understanding your own underlying structure and being willing to alter that to fit the structure of the market.

Q: *Do your students experience difficulty with getting in and out of the markets, even though they might understand the methodology that you've shown them?*

Bill: Most of them do not because during the tutorials here we actually trade. We trade very aggressively in the S&P. Once they spend three or four days here, they come out making more money, generally, than they've made before. That's sort of the clincher. But you can fairly well predict the

91

ones who are going to have more trouble, the ones who are more stuck in their ego.

I'd like to respond to something you said. I think you hit it right on the head—and that is you have to have total confidence in the way that you're trading. If you're trading and you're fearful, uptight and anxious, then I would suggest that you stop trading and start studying some more. Study the market and study yourself.

The market is the greatest teacher in the world, and I've often said that trading is the most naked psychotherapy in the whole world, if you go at it from what you can learn about yourself. You have a choice. You can go to Tibet and sit in a cave for 30 years, or you can trade the S&P for four or five days. But if you approach the market from the point of view of "What can I learn about myself as I'm trading?" then you will get a whole other viewpoint than if you approach trading from the perspective of "how much money can I make from this trade?" Good trading is much more a factor of letting go and being with the market than it is fighting the market, outsmarting the market or outsmarting the other traders.

Q: *You say letting go, but doesn't your system require that the trader pay careful attention to what the market's doing? It's a preplanned strategy, isn't it?*

Bill: Well, the strategy is preplanned, but the market will tell you exactly what to do, and it will tell you when to do it. For example, we don't spend a lot of time analyzing the market. One of our goals is that we should be able to look at any chart and know exactly what to do in less than 10 seconds. So we will come in—when we're trading the five-minute bar—and we'll analyze it. In 10 seconds we'll put on an alarm, so that if it hits—our stops are already in. But if the stops change, then the alarm hits—and what we generally do when we're day trading the S&P on a five-minute basis is trade two or three other commodities, like a currency or beans or gold or silver or sometimes the bonds, this sort of thing. So what we find is that even on a five-minute basis, we can easily, very easily, trade four different commodities and watch them all in a very leisurely fashion.

Q: *What do you think traders have to do differently in day trading as opposed to, say, position trading?*

Bill: I think most traders feel a lot more pressure in day trading, because there are more decisions per unit of time. In day trading, particularly if you're trading two or three commodities on a five-minute basis, there is no decision time. So you have to make your decisions ahead of time, and the big decision is to do what the market's telling you to do. You need an approach where your indicators are completely unambiguous, so that when the indicator hits there, it is a definite buy or sell. It's not ambiguous at all. It's not "if/maybe," it's "if this happens, then this." It has to be a very definite thing, so at that point, all of your attention is to just follow the market, without thinking.

Day trading is not a very highly intellectual process at all; it's a very simple process. And, in fact, I think that the brighter and the smarter and the more intelligent you are, probably the more difficult it is for you to make money, because what happens is that the brighter and the more intelligent you are, the more likely you are to form an opinion. For example, the S&P should go up now, and, again, if you're real bright, you will filter out all of those indicators that support your position, and you will blank out all the ones that don't, all of which gets you on the royal road to losses. What I try to do is to not get intellectual, not be real brilliant, not be real smart—just be an obedient servant.

Q: *I think the key is to create a method that's good for you and use it.*

Bill: Yes, and be committed to it and go for it.

Q: *Be committed to it until it's proven that it's not working for you anymore.*

Bill: Exactly.

Q: *What final words of advice would you offer to aspiring day traders?*

Bill: I would go easy in the beginning. I would trade only one contract. Certainly I think that day trading is well worth doing. I think it's a lot of fun. It's challenging. It will test you every day, and it's an extremely profitable way to learn a lot about who you are.

CHAPTER 7

Robin Mesch

Robin Mesch is the chief fixed-income technical analyst for Thomson Research, one of the largest providers of proprietary financial information services in the world. She is a recognized expert on Drummond Geometry. Robin authors *Trading Prophets-CBT Bonds*, a fixed-income market newsletter providing trading strategies and analysis on the 30-year Treasury bond. Robin holds a B.A. from Brown University.

Q: *How long did it take you to come up with a day trading approach that worked for you?*

Robin: I would say it is constantly evolving. We are continuously developing trading strategies because what works today isn't going to work a year from now or two years from now. We have a number of successful trading strategies that we have developed over the years that all require flexibility. It's that element of flexibility that has produced the success in our trading strategy. You know, it's the adjustments. So to answer more precisely, I would say about 12 years.

Q: *Twelve years to reach this point?*

Robin: Yes. For me it has been a developmental process. Each new technique or strategy builds on the previous one, and, of course, there's been various degrees of success along the way. Every year I hope to build on everything I've learned before.

Q: *Robin, what were some of the early experiments like?*

Robin: In the beginning our biggest struggle was picking a time frame. And I think we waffled between being very short term and then thinking, "Okay, we're going to go for the big hit." We should become long-term time frame traders.

We switched time frames a number of times in our history. And the first important learning comes when you can resolve what time frame best suits your temperament. I think the first thing we really worked on was entry and exit, finding support and resistance, coming up with a system that actually calculated levels that the market perceived as being important value levels. So that was the starting point, finding a system. And so many systems out there are good in terms of coming up with a place to buy and sell. We chose, as you know, Drummond Geometry and Market Profile, and that's what we hang our hat on. We have also done things with oscillators and MACD and stochastics.

I've studied many kinds of filters and played with a lot of different ideas. But the essence of my system is still Drummond Geometry. That's where I started. As you know from my interview in *The Outer Game of Trading* (Probus, 1994), that's how I entered the market—by learning Drummond Geometry and teaching it to someone else. And so it is the system I continue to have faith in and use.

Q: *What are some of the elements of the Drummond system?*

Robin: The basic idea is that the market itself expresses through the daily high and low and close the termination point of tomorrow's range—its high and low. So the Drummond system uses various calculations in terms of highs and lows and closes of the prior day based on averages and calculations to project what in all probability will happen tomorrow. Stochastics, for instance, are always behind; they're always a little late. They reflect what's already happened. Drummond projects what's going to happen in the future using the idea of the termination of energy of the past.

Q: *So if I understand it correctly, in broad strokes, what you're doing is setting price objectives in terms of these market swings, based on yesterday or last week or whatever time frame you are focusing on. You place price objectives in terms of where you think the market's going to go.*

Robin: Yes, except I would add, in multiple time periods.

Q: *Multiple time periods?*

Robin: Yes, using the multiple time periods is really the key. I think a lot of traders are starting to realize that you can't be a one time frame trader anymore.

Q: *When you say multiple time frames, which ones are you talking about?*

Robin: For example, if you're a day trader, you really should be looking at the weekly, monthly and quarterly charts to get your ideas of what's influencing that daily time frame. Drummond's theory uses a convergence of these termination points with multiple time periods in order to validate whether that daily support is going to work. So when you're day trading, all that information goes into the weekly, monthly and quarterly charts.

Q: *Currently, are you doing a lot of interday trading?*
Robin: Yes. That's actually where my trading is at right now.

Q: *Conceptually and in practice how do you split the day into smaller time frames?*
Robin: At a daily level we use three different interday time periods. Say, for example, I want to buy—Drummond has this whole envelope theory that we use and I write about in my market letter. So we have a daily buy level—we'll use three lower time periods, intraday time periods, to hone in at just what level to enter. Is it one tick or five? Is it going to be a few ticks below—to validate that level? And not just refine it but actually validate it.

According to this approach,if a daily support level is valid, all the other time periods have to kick in and start accumulating, which is to say the chart should be developing horizontally at this level. There are a lot of different tools to suggest we have a proper entry price. In short, we use those lower time periods to establish our maximum risk.

Q: *How did you get to the point where you could use this method?*
Robin: Well, let's see. We did some intraday work on the profile [Market Profile], and it worked really well. I still do historical testing on the intraday entry points. I've probably spent eight years on the computer looking at the stuff.

There were periods we didn't even trade. We just concentrated on computer work, massive hours. And even when you find something that looks good on paper, many times when you actually trade it, it proves not to be viable, that is, profitable. We came up early on with a system that looked good on the profile, but I couldn't execute it. I didn't feel comfortable executing it.

Q: *Well, that's a very interesting idea, the need to feel comfortable. We will talk about that a little later.*
Robin: Yes, it's important because there's not executing because of fear, not executing because you don't believe in

it, and as in my case, not executing because I just didn't feel comfortable trading it.

Q: *It seems to me, if you don't believe in it, why use it at all?*

Robin: Right, and even though it could work, it would work haphazardly—it would make gains, but the haphazardness would just run a psychological toll on you.

Q: *Of course, comfort and confidence levels absolutely skew the way you use a system.*

Robin: Exactly.

Q: *What do you feel is the key to a successful day trading system?*

Robin: That's such a good question. I want to answer it succinctly, but I know I won't be able to. Of course, there's finding your entry and exit points, coming up with a system that identifies good support and resistance levels and that doesn't take a lot of time. That could take two to three years max. Then there's using the same system over time, to figure out a good stop and how it operates under different market conditions. Then there's the overlay of the risk management, which people learn very late in their trading life. If they're still around. It's not the first thing that you think about, and the discipline of overlaying your risk management every day—no matter how juicy that trade looks and no matter what you believe about the trade—is a skill that takes many years to really inculcate into your method. That probably takes another five years. It all takes a lot of time. But that's still not the hardest part.

There's a psychology, your enthusiasm for risk, tempered with proper discipline, and an ability to act automatically—to take an instantaneous look and pick up the phone: It's the pattern, it's the signal, and you get that trade on. It's a whole other set of muscles, trader muscles, that you have to develop to be really successful. That kind of well-thought-out, conditioned fearlessness does not come easy.

Q: *Let's talk a little more about the trader's psychology.*

Robin: It's being able to execute what you see, getting the trade on, keeping the trade on and trusting that you can manage it no matter what. That ability requires a different set of muscles that you have to grow. That's why people do black box systems, because they try not to have to deal with the most difficult part of the whole process, the psychology.

The whole process is ultimately psychological. Once you have your analysis and system in place you can't say, "Well, now let's look at the hourly here. Does it look right?" You must execute!

Q: *Automatic response as a result of all the preparation?*

Robin: I've talked to a few really good traders along the way, and they have conveyed the same idea. When they're trading, they're not chatting or reading or doing something else. They're not doing some personal homework on the side while they're looking at the market. They put themselves in a chair and wait, like fishing. They just sit and wait. Even though it looks like the market is miles away from any kind of setup to buy or sell, it's just being able to sit in that chair every day and not do anything else. A lot of times, I noticed half the trades can be missed just by not being there, not being in a position to exploit opportunity. So if there's any advice to the day trader, it's to get yourself in a chair and really look at the market.

Q: *What Bob Koppel and I call "total focus."*

Robin: Total focus: 100 percent! You can't be doing anything else. It's amazing—it seems like a no-brainer—but so much of it is boring. You know, just sitting in front of the screen and looking at something, but you just have to be there!

Q: *Right. Why do you think so many people think it's impossible to day trade?*

Robin: Because it's hard! It's like anyone who's really good at something; it looks impossible to the person who isn't. We know that a ton of really good traders are out there. So it's not impossible; it's just very, very hard!

It's funny. My partner is a computer scientist. She's right up there with what I would think of as "brilliant." She's a pretty quick study. This has taken her a long time to do. She came in through the programming end, and now we're trading together. It's always encouraging when she turns to me and says, "This is really hard!"

Q: *Exactly. It's the emotional and psychological part of this thing that's so difficult.*
Robin: I think that's the biggest part.

Q: *Speaking of the emotions of trading, how do you deal with losses?*
Robin: Personally, we keep them small—we're day traders. We keep them small enough so that we don't get discouraged when we have them. We can always get in the market again. On average, we usually have about a $300 per contract tolerance on a day trade loss. If you keep the losses small, you can keep hitting the market. And keep the right psychology.

Q: *In the past, have you ever had the experience of taking a large hit?*
Robin: Oh, yeah.

Q: *What was that?*
Robin: Well, before I was trading on my own, I was trading for a company, and I just let my losses ride.

Q: *I'm sure that's never happened to anybody else!*
Robin: I did the inverse of the old trading axiom, you know?

Q: *What do you mean?*
Robin: Let your profits diminish; let your losses rise?
It was in the S&P. I think the Fed came in and eased, tightened or did some such thing, and I was in the opposite direction. It happened so fast! I think I went up to get a cup of tea, and the next thing I know I was in deep trouble. I

had that king-of-the-mountain syndrome, you know. I'm doing so well, I can't possibly get hurt.

Q: *I know you've read* The Innergame of Trading *where we talk about euphoric trading.*
Robin: Right. I was reading in your book about the trader who said the feeling is like following a simple internal recipe: Crawl up stairs, stand on window sill, jump to concrete 33 floors below!

Q: *It all amounts to the same thing, you know. We become invulnerable in our own minds.*
Robin: Yeah, there's a lot of things to master in day trading. You have to break it down. I think that is a good place to start. Breaking it down, so you know exactly how you have to think and act.

Q: *I'm not going to allow you to escape from my previous question. So what happened next?*
Robin: The first thing I did was try to find other people who lost money on that day too!

Q: *Misery loves company!*
Robin: I found some of them, and you know, we all started doing the pacing routine. We all paced together around the room. But here is the remarkable thing: We were still in the trade. So I just kept talking to myself over and over again until I did what always happens in this situation. You buy the high and now you're out. Hopefully, you've paid the market for an important lesson!

Q: *I think people who are reading this will find comfort in knowing that successful traders have experienced the same things they are going through.*
Robin: That's how it usually goes. Just when you cannot take the pain any longer, you get out and establish the high for the day in the S&P 500.

Q: *So how did you move on from that experience to your next trade?*

Robin: In the old days, it would take a long time for me to get back on track, just because the losses in dollar terms were so significant. The people I was trading with would say, "Oh, I'm losing a million dollars today, 3 million dollars." It was because they were calloused or seasoned that I really respected their judgment at the time, and for me, it was all pretty new—having to deal with that kind of size. It would take months to recuperate. I'm not kidding. I mean, I was at the point that I wouldn't second-guess myself, getting out of trades too early, keeping my stops too tight, those kinds of things.

Q: *How about now?*

Robin: Well, now, I realize, especially in this kind of market, that for day traders, you can't go for the kill. It is not the right mentality. Wrong, wrong, wrong, wrong, wrong. You should go in with the attitude to make a living every day. I think that's the great thing about day trading. There are daily opportunities in the market. You don't have to go for the kill. I'm happy with making money every day and maintaining a risk level that I am comfortable with.

Q: *How do you deal with the profits?*

Robin: You know, there you go, you always ask the tough questions! I'm working on that issue of always maximizing profits tempered with not going for the kill. How do you deal with profits? I think that's a little bit more of an issue for a swing and a position trader. For the day trader, if you've gotten in at the right point, you know, the market's going to tell you when you're right. You're right very quickly, right enough to know that you should stay with it. And the best strategy, when a market goes your way quickly, the best strategy is to move your stops up right away. In my experience, the really big moves happen really fast, and so that's how we deal with it. We move our stops up and stay with it until we're stopped out or the market reaches our price objective.

Q: *Do you have any feelings about the money you leave on the table?*

Robin: It's a killer. It really is. I mean, yesterday, we bought five ticks off the low on the S&P, and we knew it was going up. We got in, started fiddling with the market and got out too soon. We put some money on the table, but we didn't stay true to our game plan.

Q: *Lost focus.*

Robin: What about you, how do you deal with it?

Q: *Well, personally, it's something I have to deal with constantly, because I do a combination of trading. I do a lot of day trading, but I'm also running programs that are swing and longer-term trading. So trying to wear those hats at times becomes difficult.*

I believe when you put day trades on, it's almost mandatory that you never change the time frame with which you're operating, because to do anything else is the worst thing that you can do. If we think we have a swing trade or an entry place that is both a day trade possibility and a swing trade possibility, then we obviously have multiple contracts on, and we start to take money off the table as the market develops. And then for the swing trade, if we get a nice strong close in our favor, we just stay overnight and let the market tell us what to do next. Trading in more than one time frame is very difficult. You must be very disciplined, and you have to have programs that are so defined that you really don't have to worry about mixing time frames up. One thing I think that hurts people when they try to day trade is what they think about all of these other issues instead of focusing in on the day trade.

Robin: That's true, and that's why I don't think leaving money on the table is as big an issue when you're day trading, because you aren't going for the kill as a day trader.

Q: *In your opinion, how is long-term trading different from day trading?*

Robin: Position traders have to have a lot of money. They have to have a really good system that's directional. It is a help that their system is directionally oriented, meaning the strong point of their system has to predict where the market's going rather than identifying precise market location. And that's not what my system is. It's much more oriented to price and trade location. Of course, we do stuff with direction, but location is our major focus.

Position traders also have to be thinking about quarterly and yearly time frames. Everything else is just noise. So position traders really have to be thinking in much broader strokes, the big picture. But still the day trader has to know the chart.

We haven't been selling the S&P, even though you could have made lots of money on the sell side. We haven't touched the sell side. Why? Because the money's been easier to make on the buy side. It's been hard to make it on the sell side. You have had to work twice as hard in the S&P to be right on the sell side than on the buy side. That's a good definition of a bull market. So my point is this: You have to know what's going on in the market. What is the general context of your trade?

Q: *What recommendations would you make to traders who are having difficulty with the day trading process?*

Robin: You really have to force yourself to put the trade on. There's a period of, like, not paper trading. Well, some people call it that, but it's really just observing and building up the confidence. But managing the trade is an art that you can learn only by putting the trade on, by actually doing it. You do develop a skill for managing a bad trade, a skill that is necessary to be a good trader. It's not just a stop, because lots of time we get out before our stop is hit. You have to know before you get into a trade what has to happen. So even if you're not in at a good trade location or even if you didn't do your usual discipline of entry, you should always know what now has to unfold next. And this is the monitoring phase of the management. In short, you have to have a set of rules after entry of what the market has to do after you're in.

People leave that step out. They get in. They put in a stop. They know where they want to get out but don't concentrate on managing the trade.

Q: *They become passive about the trade.*
Robin: Yes. That's right. You don't want to be too involved. But you have to have certain time objectives or marking points. If we're right, then this or that should occur; but if it doesn't, then we have to reevaluate and most likely get out.

Q: *It sounds like you're setting up criteria for the market to behave in a certain way, and if it doesn't, if it disappoints you, you get out.*
Robin: Right.

Q: *With a small profit or whatever.*
Robin: Right, or a scratch. Psychologically, it's important to not feel like you're copping out by getting out.

Q: *Right. I think that'll resonate with a lot of people also.*
Robin: Yes, I'm sure it will. I would like to add something: Find a good mentor. Study with someone who's genuine and who really can teach you something. Look around to find someone who can trade and has traded successfully.

Remember also, depths over time equal growth. The more you keep delving into the markets, the more you will grow in your understanding about how they work. It requires perseverance and dedication.

Q: *You mean we're going to leave the readers with the idea that commitment, hard work and focus are going to help them get ahead?*
Robin: Absolutely, that's what will give them the edge. Unfortunately, most people don't have the staying power to go the distance.

Q: *That's right. If you want to be a top trader, it's like preparing to be a long distance runner. Marathon man and woman!*

Robin: Don't lose your focus! Yeah. I mean, you have to be somewhat smart, but you have to do it.

Q: *Well, we know we're dealing with smart people. Most people who entertain the idea of our business generally are smart people and are drawn to it for very intelligent reasons. It's in the performing that changes the whole picture.*

PART FOUR

The Top Traders

CHAPTER 8

David Silverman

David Silverman is a long-term member of the Chicago Mercantile Exchange, where he was an active floor trader in the currency pits. He is currently serving as a member of the Board of Directors of the Chicago Mercantile Exchange and is a partner in M & S Trading, a Commodities Trading Advisor. David holds a B.A. with honors in History from the University of Chicago.

Q: *How long did it take you to develop a day trading approach that worked?*

David: I started to trade when I was 22 years old, and it probably took me at least two, maybe three, years till I had any degree of success. One of the reasons it took so long was that I was a novice at business, and I wasn't quite sure how to make my way in the world of trading in general: You know, all the little practical things that you don't even think about until you have to! Once the first year of paying dues was past, maybe it took another year or year-and-a-half till I actually was thinking about trading all the time.

Q: *David, how would you characterize those early years?*

David: I read virtually every single book that was ever written about trading at the time. I experimented with every conceivable idea and system. They didn't really have computer systems back then, but I tried all the systems that so-called market gurus were recommending. I think I spent some of my money—and, mind you, I didn't have too much at the time—on buying market recommendations, thinking that was the easy way to be a successful trader. But I learned real quickly, and I lost a lot of money doing that! So finally I realized that I had to find my own niche, and I decided to do it for myself.

I remember there was one system—I convinced a friend to go in on this system with me. We traded it for quite a while, and we both lost so much money on it! It's ridiculous! He still makes fun of me about it to this day.

I think it was called the "congestion phase system." Years later, when I learned how to program and had more experience, I realized that there really was some sense to it. But the point is that it is not for me! You had to look for 30 or 40 different patterns. They were looking at market closes, and if, for instance, the market closed up three days in a row, you were supposed to go home short on the close. Each pattern was actually mapped out for you. And you see, the worst thing that happened to me was that the first trade I took was successful! I think I made 60 ticks overnight in the deutsche mark. I thought to myself, "This is it." So I began thinking to myself, "I'm 23 years old. I'm going to be a millionaire in the next six months." I had it all planned so that after a while I could just take it easy. The problem is after that I don't think I ever had another winning trade with the congestive phase system.

Q: *Why do you think it didn't work?*

David: I think part of the problem was that I didn't really understand what the method was all about. And like I say, in retrospect, I think that there's actually some sense to the approach. There are ways, as you know, to make money fading—by fading the market—which is essentially what the system was all about. The essential point is that the system was not right for me. I was in no position financially to be putting on the kinds of positions I did and taking the sort of risk that fading the market entailed. Also I came to believe, and it's probably good I learned this fact early in my career, that unless you totally understand the nature of what you're doing, without qualification, you're just shooting craps! I mean, occasionally there's a certain degree of comfort that you get by putting your lot in with someone who you think is more successful than you or smarter than you. But in general, I'm very much against black box sorts of systems or just accepting something on face value without giving it really a thorough and rigorously tested analysis. Trading in this age of powerful computers, just about anybody is in a position to test things in a relatively simple way. There's really no excuse for not testing something out. And of course, it's the only way you will know if it has some validity. If you don't, you're just looking for the easy way out, and I don't think there's an easy way out in trading. It took me many years to come to that conclusion!

Q: *You mean it takes hard work.*

David: It takes real hard work, and it doesn't ever stop! I say this because (1) the markets are changing all the time; and (2) while there might be some general precepts that apply to the long-term market, on a day-to-day basis, practically speaking for day trading, these precepts are not necessarily relevant. I think, for day trading purposes, some of the traditional ways that people look at the market are not necessarily helpful, and you must appreciate that.

It might be a time of low volatility; it might be a time of high volatility. A system that works well on the long side might not work well on the short side, for some reason, and then suddenly it may turn around and reverse. I suppose this raises the question of how good any system is over a long period of time. I think, over time, however, you must recognize as a day trader that markets change routinely. You have to be very adaptable—much more so than as a long-term trader.

Q: *I certainly would agree with that. You described one system that you tried and later abandoned. Any others?*

David: As I said before, I bought a number of systems over time but none that I spent a great deal of money on. It was more a question of wasting time. Trying to find the simple answer rather than finding out for myself what works.

Q: *Early on, were there any systems that you developed for yourself that didn't work, and if so, why didn't they work?*

David: I developed some systems using Trade Station by Omega Research, but to date I haven't found anything that's better than my own intuition about the market.

I would like to say something about the problems associated with slippage. When you're trading on the floor, slippage is not a big problem, but once you go off the floor you recognize very quickly what a big concern it actually is. I make a point of using only the best brokers in every pit—only the people who I think really know what they're doing, who are well connected and who can really get the best prices in the pit. I want only the brokers who are well skilled and well positioned, and even so, I still have problems with slippage. And so, to get back to your question, I've found that some of the systems I developed have ended up being extremely less profitable than they appeared when the computer spit out the numbers, primarily because of the slippage. I also think, quite frankly, that there probably aren't that many great systems out there!

The market is extremely efficient, and I think that for a day trader, it's very hard to find consistently efficient systems. If you're a longer-term trader, I believe deeply that there are a lot of good systems that you can find or even that you can buy. I certainly don't mean to denigrate the work of long-term traders. But in general, it's much easier to follow a trend than it is to develop a day trading system that's going to be in and out and profitable on a consistent basis.

I guess it's like they say about football, you should choose a running game over a passing game. When passing, two out of the three things that can happen are negative, but when running the ball, only one out of two are negative. So I think it's kind of like that—the more decisions you make, the more chances there are that you can screw up. If you then add in slippage, clearly the more chances you have for slippage, the more negative the impact on the system. And so I think that in trending markets, you can use systems to great effect in ways that don't practically play out when you day trade.

Q: *As you know, it's my view that any method we use in order to deal with the markets effectively becomes a system for us. It need not be a mechanical device in which to enter or exit markets. You said earlier that you're an intuitive trader. What are some tools that you use to help you make day trading decisions?*

David: I would venture to say that my tools are probably a lot different from the majority of indicators that are used by people who day trade off of the trading floor. Having been on the trading floor for 13 years has been an invaluable experience. The intuition you develop not only with respect to what the market itself is doing but with respect to body language of the people around you, the noise level, the degree of hysteria or lack thereof is incredibly useful when trading off the floor. I think that even if I never were to spend another day on the trading floor, I'm still going to be forever influenced by those sorts of stimuli, and they give me a sense of the market.

Let me try to be more precise. Currently, I am trading currencies. I hear on the floor there's a guy standing right by the pit. On the phone I'm listening to the quotes, the noise level of the pit; that's something I find invaluable. Occasionally I find myself kind of feeling naked when I trade something like soybeans. Because I don't have the same feel for this market, they don't know me at the desk, and they just kind of "tell" me what's there. I might tell them to go to the market, and that's it. In the currencies, where I know the market inside out, I feel a physical connection, whether it's through hearing or by actually feeling what it's like being present in the pit. As a matter of fact, at the exchange, we've been talking about putting cameras over the pit and broadcasting it through satellites so that people can actually kind of get what one trader called "The Wow" of being on the exchange. For me those feelings are key.

I think these feelings are part and parcel of my intuition. It's these feelings that allow me to be successful at day trading. Many traders, I guess, try to go with the trend as they define it. But personally I find that more often than not, I'm usually trying to find the place where the trend is about to turn around.

I'm trying to figure out where is the good place for the next swing. You can figure it out even though you're going against the short-term run. I'm thinking about where is a good place for there to be a turnaround and have the market come back 50 percent. It just broke 100 points. You know, maybe it's ready now to rally back that 40 or 50 points. I get real nervous about running after a long running move. I'm a lot less nervous about finding a place to get in where I think the momentum may be turning. These have been really my best trades over time. I mean, the biggest days I've had by far have been days where I've been able to discern where the market's momentum was petering out, and it could have gone the opposite way. Of course, many times I have gotten run over when I've stopped in front of a train. But I try to keep my numbers small enough so that if I'm wrong about my decisions, even in a worst-case scenario, I'm not going to get hurt! After 13 years, I can say I've never been in a situation where I've lost so much on any one trade that I can't come back tomorrow!

Q: *What do you think are the specific keys to successful day trading?*

David: I think it's really important, even though you may be looking for moves within a trend, for example, to know where the major support and resistance points are. I am particularly technically oriented. I mean, I know where all the major support and resistance points are in the markets that I'm trading. Even if I'm going to be trading very actively in between those points, I think some of the best opportunities will end up coming when the markets get to those specific extremes. I think therefore that it's crucially important to acquaint yourself with the major support and resistance. I think it's important to try to keep an eye—even though this is a traditionally longer-term approach—on what's happening with respect to the volume and open interest. I would also add volatility. I think it gives you a sense of who's playing in the market and what's really happening.

Of course, it goes without saying that it's really important to use conservative money management principles. One thing I learned when I started trying to develop systems over the last couple of years is that the money management is the crucial element in day trading. You could write a system that says: "Buy the market when it rains, and sell when it stops raining." And you know what? You could probably make money with that system, if you had good money management techniques. Although let me be emphatic: This is no recommendation! It almost doesn't matter what the idea is. You have to make sure that you are putting on positions that make sense, relative to your total equity and to what you are expecting to get out of the trade. And I have done a great deal of testing on different systems, and this testing convinced me that the idea is not anywhere near as important as the money management principles. You never want to be in a position, no matter how strongly you feel about a trade, that the trade may put you out of business!

Now maybe that sounds extreme, but I know lots of people—I'm sure you do also—who have gotten themselves in exactly that position. All of a sudden they had a 300 contract position, and the next thing you know they're in the exchange membership department selling their seat, or, you know, they're in big trouble. And so if I've done anything successfully over the last 13 years, I think it's to keep myself out of that sort of situation by exercising sound money management. I should add that there have been plenty of times when I've gone home shaking my head about how much more I could have made if I just would have taken a larger risk. I remember one trade that occurred a number of years ago in the deutsche marks. It was on the close, and an order came in, I think, in the third or fourth option out. It was for 1,100 contracts on the close, and the order filler took the spread out of line by 50 points. Intuitively, I knew that this was a chance to make $700,000. Nevertheless, I could not bring myself to do the whole 1,100 contracts. I bought a hundred and made 50 points a contract. It was a terrific trade, but I went home beating myself over the head. But you see I did the right thing! You have to be consistent in how you approach the markets. You can't make exceptions! You can't say to yourself, in reality, "Well, I'm not an 1,100 contract trader. I'm a 100 contract trader. But this is just such a good trade that I can't pass it up!" There may have been a real good reason why the D-mark was 50 points out of line, and maybe I was going to walk in the next day and that spread was going to be 100 points or 200 "out of line." You know, these are the sorts of things that I think people should attune themselves to, namely, the need to consistently stick to a winning approach. Still, even to this day, I think about that trade!

Q: *It sounds like you're still thinking about it!*

David: Well, it sticks out of all the thousands of trades one makes over the years. But I think that in all seriousness, it's very important to have a plan, to be consistent in how you employ it and not to make exceptions. The exceptions will lay you away!

Another thing I would like to talk about is taking a loss. You must learn to lose. You must understand that since you make a lot of trades, your winning percentage may be very low, as opposed to a long-term trader's percentage. I mean, I think you could really write a system with a wide enough stop that probably comes close to 100 percent profitability; however, that's not what day traders do. You have to become inured to the fact that you're going to be wrong a lot. That's what makes day trading so hard! In fact, that was the essential lesson that turned my day trading around. When I went to school, I was a straight-A student. That's how we define success in grammar school, high school and college. You know, I was always at the top of my class. Then I came into the exchange and quickly learned that maybe five out of every ten trades were losers on a good day. Well, initially I felt like a complete failure. That was part of the maturation process. I had to learn that knowing how to lose and to move on could make you very successful. Losing is just part of the game.

Q: *You have been very successful at day trading over a rather long period of time. We also know many other people who day trade very effectively on a consistent basis. Why do you think there are so many people who think day trading is impossible, that it is essentially a fruitless enterprise?*

David: I think part of it has to do with the fact that most people are lazy. They really have an unrealistic perspective about futures trading. They believe that since you have a 50-50 chance of being right when you buy a market—it's either going to go up or it's going to go down—that it must be simple.

You know, if you were to go into a hospital emergency room and begin to perform brain surgery on somebody who just got shot in the head, you would have a 0 percent chance of being successful at that! I mean all of us would readily admit that. We wouldn't even know where to start. But the novice trader opens an account with a couple of thousand dollars and feels he or she has a great shot at making money, feels it's just that simple. And you and I know it's just not that easy, even if you find a system that's 60 percent or 70 percent or 90 percent effective, because you're not just talking about numbers that a computer is spitting out. The weak link to any trading system is the trader. It's extremely hard to make money trading, and people should recognize that fact going in. They should not harbor misconceptions that it's something they can do in their spare time, without enduring a lot of pain, monetary as well as psychological. It's really one of the hardest professions that I can think of. Everyone I know in the business who is successful has worked very hard. It takes hard work and discipline. It does not just happen!

Q: *We know that people look for systems and look for any other thing that they can grab hold of to assure success. From your point of view, how important is psychology when it comes to short-term trading?*

David: Well, particularly because in day trading you make so many trades, I think positive psychology is critical. It is much more important than for the long-term trader. Every time you put a trade on, a little bit of you gets torn out. As I said before, you have to learn how to take losses; you may have to take a series of losses in a row. You must feel at these times that you're not a bad person; you're not incompetent. Remember, only if you have some degree of confidence in your program, whether it's mechanical or intuitive, along with sound money management principles, will you be successful at trading. Now if you find out after a period of time that it's not a good program and it has to be changed, well then, change it! Of course, that's if you still have some money left.

If you have sound money management principles, you know, as I said before, there are a million ways to make money trading! I think people really serious about trading should determine how much money they can commit, how much time, and seriously think about a time line, how much they're prepared to put in, both financially and emotionally, and then give it a good run. Don't say after the first ten trades, "Oh, the hell with this!" or "I'm just going to try to put on 30 contracts to make it all back." I mean, even if you're right, it'll be like me trying to make money on the congestion phase system. It's luck, not brains, and in the long run it won't be of any value to you. It'll certainly be of negative value to you, because it will convince you that you have something good when you really don't have anything at all.

Q: *What do you think the optimum psychology is for success in day trading?*

David: I think it's self-confidence, because you have to deal with all those losses. You have to have confidence, not only in your program but in yourself. You have to be very patient, because you can have long periods of time where you don't do well. Every trader who's been around for a while has gone through these stretches. It wears you down. It impinges on every aspect of your life.

Perhaps it's no different than any other profession. Anybody who's having a hard time at the office comes home and takes it out on the family. I'm not entirely sure it's more so here, but in one respect it is. Trading gives you immediate and constant feedback. It's always right in your face. You get a daily statement, or it may be a trade-by-trade statement of how you're doing. I mean, if a lawyer is trying a case, the thing could go on for a year, and there may be ups and downs, winning the case, then losing the case, whatever! But with trading, especially if you're going through a period of losses, every single time you make a losing trade, it feels like a little piece of you gets torn out, financially and emotionally. And then as if that were not bad enough, you have fewer chips to play with!

Q: *How do you handle the losses?*

David: When I was younger, I handled them very badly. I think that I let them creep into my life outside of trading. I would very frequently have dreams about trading. I used to have one terrible dream about where I put on a trade, and it was a winner. It was a big trade—maybe the biggest trade I ever had on! Now here's the part that is absolutely hysterical. I'm trying to take a profit, and nobody hears my order, nobody's listening to me. I am invisible. Everybody's oblivious to me, and meanwhile the market starts going against me. The market goes against me, and now this trade that was a fantastic winner turns into just an enormous loser. But there's more! The bell rings, and I have to go home with the trade. At that point my alarm would go off, and I'd wake up in a sweat. Believe me when I tell you I would have dreams like that all the time. But even worse than dreams—which, you know, we can sit around and laugh about—was my attitude. I would go home and beat myself up over trades, even over winning trades: I didn't have enough on, or I didn't take enough out of it. This type of thinking is very negative. It was negative for me; it was very negative for my relationship with my family and my friends outside work. Also, I had an extremely bad habit when I was younger, when I was around traders outside of the market in a social situation, to talk about nothing but trading. Now that I think about it, I was lucky my wife was never near any sharp instruments, because that used to drive her up the wall! But like I said, that was when I was younger. I mean, I think I've gotten away from that now! But that is all part of the hard psychological issues that are part of trading.

Q: *How did you resolve that issue?*

David: My wife was extremely helpful to me, because it wasn't healthy, and I would say the majority of traders I know have exhibited this sort of behavior or, you know, are plagued by it if they haven't resolved it. You see, it was that I recognized that as a problem. I mean, it's money, and it's important, it's your profession, but if it's going to make you unhappy outside of the confines of your trading, then really what's the point?

Q: *In what ways did a negative psychology affect your decision making?*

David: There were days when I would be coming off a big winning day or winning streak, and that would influence me in a negative way in terms of how I would approach the next day's trading. I was totally caught up in the emotion. I would say, "Oh, I'm hot; I've really got to push it," when maybe there wasn't anything to do. I discarded my money management principles because I thought I was on fire. Or the other way, if I were going through a period of bad times, I might go into a shell and start to question the validity of my program, lose my self-confidence and become paralyzed.

There were plenty of days or periods of time in my career where I would become paralyzed and be unable to function. There were trades that I knew I should be making, but instead I would just let them pass by because I was afraid.

As I said before, I think you have to have a lot of self-confidence to avoid falling in those negative traps of fear and paralysis because they're very real.

Q: *At the very least, it would seem to me that recognizing negative emotions as a problem is a huge head start.*

David: Yes, as I said, my wife has been very helpful to me. It's vital to acknowledge that these pressures are infringing on your life. Sometimes, even after all these years, I find myself falling into the same traps, but hopefully, you know, I see it in the right context and am able to pull myself out before it gets too bad.

Q: *Can you describe your trading method? What I'm interested in is how you approach markets. How do you identify opportunity?*

David: I said at the start of this interview that I know the major support and resistance points in the markets that I'm trading. Accordingly, I know the general bands within which I expect the market to trade in a single session or over a period of sessions. In addition, I read four or five newspapers a day, and I use CQG, while I go through all of the news stories in the morning before I even begin trading. I trade, as you know, currencies mostly, so I have to check what's happened overnight in London, especially in the last year or so, because it's become increasingly important to pay attention to that. In short, all of this is the preliminary preparation. And then once I'm at my desk, I'm trying to, as I said earlier, look for places where I think the strength or weakness in a market is beginning to dissipate. I'm trying to identify where in the market people are going to feel that they have to rush to the door to get out. Generally, you get real quick gratification. I like that. I like seeing the quick reversal. I don't like putting on a trade that's going against the trend and then sitting an hour or two with it, because that's an indication to me that my analysis is probably flawed, and it probably isn't an area where the market is turning around.

Also, depending on the volatility, the band within which I look to fade the market changes. You know, at a time when it's not very volatile, you may be looking for very small moves, but in a time of great volatility, for instance, a fast market or a major report, you really have to widen your bands. I'm not going to fade every 10- or 15-point rally in the D-mark. The market now has to move 70 or 80 ticks before I will fade it, but on the other side of the coin, you get a much bigger payoff when you're right! Of course, during these times, it's more dangerous if you're wrong, but again, with sound money management principles, you should be able to take even a whole series of losses doing that, because when you're right, you will capture 40, 50 or 60 ticks very quickly.

Now let's say you have a situation where the market is above its 50-day moving average, 20-day moving average and 10-day moving average. Most people would probably say that's a long-term up trend, and so let's take this scenario. Imagine over the past three or four trading sessions, the market hasn't exploded, but it's gone up every single day just a little bit. I'm really uncomfortable about buying a market like that. That's the kind of market where I really want to look for a spot to sell. I want to find the area where the market gets soft, because whoever bought it up to then is going to start to get nervous. They're either going to say, "I've got to take this profit now," or if they were unlucky enough to do the trade that I just said I don't want to do, they're going to be rushing for the exit because they're going to say, "Oh, God. I got in at the top." So if you're smart enough and fortunate enough to get in, in about that area, that's a place where, as I say, you get a really nice spot to capitalize on crowd mentality.

I want to be categorical about one thing. I'm not suggesting this is the only way to do it. I think it's something that I'm comfortable with. I know plenty of people who would think that selling a market like that is absolutely insane, and intellectually I might agree with them. But I've been able to do what I do successfully for many years. I really find the number of times when I chase a market as opposed to fading the market is small, and the amount of the success I've had chasing the market or going with the trend is minimal in comparison to taking the other side.

Q: *Can you give me an example of a time or two that you had to deal with a significant market loss where you might have done all the "right" things but still encountered an equity loss?*

David: I used to be an extremely active scalper in the pit. On some days I would trade 1,000 round turns. When you're trading like that, you're usually standing near to the order flow. And the order flow, in general, tends to chase the market. During fast markets and busy markets, generally, if the market's going up, there'll be a lot of buy stops at some point. If the market's going down, there'll be a lot of sell stops. In these situations, the larger floor traders tend to take the other side of these orders.

These orders may be from CTAs. They may be from institutions. They may be from the smartest people in the world who, in the short run, don't care what price they pay but know that they want to be long deutsche marks if it's going up or short deutsche marks if it's going down. Scalpers, on the other hand, have no interest whatsoever in long-term direction of the D-marks. Their only interest is where it's going until they get out of that trade, which hopefully will be a matter of seconds, and that it be profitable.

Q: *That goes for the person who's day trading as well, doesn't it?*

David: Exactly. You really have no interest in six months down the road, or even tomorrow. The down side to all of this as a scalper is that while you have people paying up to you, giving you your price, if you are wrong, you can really take some big losses very quickly. When I was very active in the pit, there were a few times when I took trades that were really too large and probably unwise. I took them, not because I thought the market was really getting soft, but rather because someone was willing to pay my price. Once you get whacked a few times doing that, you realize that you have to be very judicious about setting your price. It taught me to really look for the soft spots, rather than just say, "Oh, I can set the price, so therefore this must be a good trade."

Q: *How do you deal with the profits?*

David: When I was younger, I attributed way too much importance to the fact that I was able to trade profitably. I think that, especially when someone who's young has a degree of success trading, they tend to equate their self-worth with their net worth, and they begin to think that they're invincible or they've beaten the market, and that this is somehow important in the great scheme of things. As I've gotten older, I try to treat my profits with equanimity and not exaggerate them beyond the fact that they can just pay my bills, put some money in the bank and get me through to the next trading day. Truly, it's very difficult sometimes when you're doing well, because you naturally assume that it's never going to stop. You convince yourself that you can do this forever, but it's not only good advice to the novice that it is hard to trade and that you can't be lazy; it's even more important to the traders who have had success because if they start to let their guard down and don't adapt to changing markets, they will get caught. The market is very efficient at doing this to all of us. And so, really, when you're having good times and are being profitable, it is just the time when you should be doing some serious analysis about your trading. Really, that's the best time. No one wants to do it then, but that is absolutely the essential time to be self-critical to see whether what you're doing is really the right thing.

Q: *Why do you think most people are not successful at day trading?*

David: Again, I think a lot of people I've met are lazy. They don't work hard enough at it, and it's very hard. Most people are very comfortable with not pressing and not doing all the things that are required to succeed. They want things to come easily, and this is not a profession where that's going to happen. But more than that, I think, is the whole issue we discussed earlier, namely, taking losses. If you have only 40 percent or 50 percent winning trades or even less, it's extremely difficult to deal with that. You begin to think sometimes that you're not good at this, that you'll never be good at this! You know, in baseball, if you hit safely three out of ten times, it gets you $5 million a year. There are people in this business who are right three times out of ten times and make lots of money. I think Richard Dennis said once that he makes 90 percent of his money on 5 percent or 10 percent of his trades. I think we would all agree the man has made lots of money!

Q: *This baseball player you referred to who gets paid $5 million a year, who gets three hits out of ten at bats, you know this player has to deal with the issue of the other seven times as well.*

David: I have a friend who's a CTA who trades options, and his program essentially is buying out-of-the-money puts and calls. That's what he does. He's got positions on in 25 different markets, betting on volatility. That's his game, and there are times when the markets are not volatile. Now he trades markets across a very broad spectrum to try to diversify. It's a very clever tactic, but at least theoretically, all 25 of those markets could have a period of no volatility, and he could be 0 for 25 for a period of time. He knows that's one of the pitfalls, and he's within his model, his intuitive model, which is to say he's allowed for that possibility. And so that's really the important thing, that you have to be comfortable and confident in your program, and you have to be willing to deal with the fact that it's not always going to work right.

Q: *I know we have touched on a little of this earlier; what are some other differences that you see between larger-term trading and day trading?*

David: Well, again, a position trader isn't going to have to make as many decisions. So I think you have to be comfortable with dealing with more variables. You have to be willing to make decisions automatically with precision in a way a long-term trader generally doesn't have to. You have to work with much tighter stops. I mean, most day traders I know have to work with infinitely tighter stops than long-term traders do. I think—maybe I should have made this point before—I think stops are very important. I think that, you know, it's okay to have intuitive stops. And maybe as a tactic, some people feel that actually having the stop in the pit or with your broker is not a smart way to trade. Personally, I don't put much credence in that point of view.

I think that there's a certain liberating factor when you have chosen an exit point, or for that matter, a stop as an entry point into the market. It's liberating in the sense that the decision-making process that's tied to your model or program is now automatically acted upon. I think one thing that's very hard for traders, especially novice traders, is that they're retentive in the decisions they make. At the moment that they make it, it might seem like a brilliant decision, a right decision. It makes complete sense within the scope of what they're trying to do. And the moment that the market gets anywhere close, they get cold feet! I remember we used to mercilessly make fun of this one guy in the pit who would always bid and offer one point below the offer and offer one point above the bid, and in five years, I don't think we ever saw this guy make a trade! Sadly, he just wasn't capable of pulling the trigger. I think it's really important, particularly if you're not a mechanical trader, that you put your orders in ahead of time.

Also, tactically I think it makes a lot of sense to have an idea where you want to get out, where you want to get in. And so I use stops every time I trade. I mean, I just can't imagine a situation where I would put a trade on, or want to put a trade on, where I wouldn't have either an exit point that's covered by a stop or an entry point that's covered by a stop.

Q: *Any final words of wisdom?*

David: I would say try to avoid the impact of the emotional highs and lows. I touched on it earlier. You know, the money comes and goes very quickly in trading, and hopefully you'll make more than you lose, but truly it's not such a big deal. I mean, presuming you can make a living at it, if you didn't make a little bit more than you thought you should have, the world isn't going to come to an end. And if you don't put your whole lot on the line and have good trading discipline, then you're always going to be able to come back for the next trading sessions. I think if you approach it with a sense of equanimity and don't get too excited when you're winning or losing, you certainly can be successful. If nothing else, you'll be a healthier human being.

CHAPTER 9

Larry Rosenberg

Larry Rosenberg is a long-term member of the Chicago Mercantile Exchange and is a past Chairman of the Board of Directors.

Larry was an active floor trader for many years and continues to trade successfully for his own account from on and off the exchange floor.

Q: *Could you describe how you developed your day trading approach?*

Larry: That's an interesting question. I started trading at the Board of Trade in 1961. My first year as a floor trader was my only losing year in 35 years of trading. I lost a couple of dollars, but my trading system evolved. So I guess the answer to your question is that it evolved through trial and error.

Q: *Early on, what was the learning process like?*

Larry: Well, one thing I know that didn't work for me back then was charting. There were no computer systems then, and charting just didn't appeal to me. I was an intuitive trader, and I developed a sense for the market from being in the pits.

I traded all the grain pits—corn, beans, etc. You develop a sense of timing. I guess it's an educated reaction. I think it's more auditory than anything else. The sound of a bear market has a different "voice" than a bull market. So you develop this auditory sense, and that's basically how I developed into a trader. I didn't use any specific formula, any systems, but like all traders whose experience develops, I think that certain things become ingrained, and, you know, you begin forming a chart in your head.

One thing I did learn early in my career: When I get into a position, I am not as much concerned about where I take the profit, as when to "get out." I always have a mental stop and am ready to act on it.

Q: *That seems to be a common theme with former floor traders.*

Larry: Well, I think for anyone who survives, that's the answer. You have to know what your risk is; you can't leave it open-ended. You know, giving back profits is not a happy situation, but it beats the hell out of ballooning losses! I guess, if anything, that's probably what made me a successful trader. I developed that discipline, and I stuck with it. Some of the best trades I ever made in my 35 years on the floor were scratches. Take a position, and it's no good; I'm out right away! I wasn't comfortable. I'll take those trades every time!

Q: *It doesn't matter what happened afterwards.*
Larry: I couldn't care less.

Q: *It could have been the right thing to do or . . .*
Larry: For example, if it was a buy and I scratched it, it's not the right thing to do, so I'll pay higher and buy it

back. For those traders who are on the floor, that's why you're there.

Q: *That's true, but you're not on the floor now. Does some of this relate to off-floor trading?*
Larry: Oh, yes. Absolutely. I'm a disciplined person, you know, and I think that's very important. So whatever system you use will work as long as you're disciplined.

Q: *And the method has . . .*
Larry: Viability. Exactly.

Q: *Well, you said . . .*
Larry: I think the big key is discipline. Now when I'm off the floor, any time I establish a trade—if I put in an order—I know where my stop belongs, where I'm wrong, and that discipline carries over to the entire process. Obviously, I can't place it as a floor trader; my parameters have expanded, but I think that is such an essential part of trading. Also, when I make a trade, I have some idea of what my profit objective is. I allow that part of it to be flexible. The market gets there, and I can decide—whatever. But one thing that isn't flexible and is never expanded is my stop point. For example, assuming I have a long position, I might raise the stop if the market's going with me, but I'll never lower it!

Q: *You said that your first year at trading wasn't profitable; it was kind of a learning experience. What did you do differently after the first year to make you profitable?*
Larry: First, I think it was getting in tune with the market and the trading environment. As you know, it's a unique atmosphere to say the least. Second, I developed trading discipline and learned how to stop myself out of the market.

Q: *Recently most of your time has been spent off the floor, right?*
Larry: All of it.

Q: *How has your trading method evolved?*

Larry: Well, it's interesting because it has been a learning experience coming off the floor. It took me, basically, a couple of years to really learn how to trade off the floor. It took me almost a year to unlearn many tactics that work downstairs but not upstairs.

Q: *You didn't have the auditory?*

Larry: Now it's all visual. Auditory has nothing to do with it! Sometimes it was gut reactions, which work fine in the pit but are useless in front of a screen. In fact, some pit tactics are really dangerous up here. But what I've learned in essence is that discipline remains. It's critical. As important as it is on the floor, it's more important off the floor, but I have to do a little more homework at night as a screen trader. I go over the numbers, and I plan strategies for what I want to do the next day.

So I've had to learn different things. The main thing, though, I will say again is the discipline. I can't emphasize that point strongly enough. Also, let me say that part of the learning experience was becoming comfortable in this environment. It's quite a difference to go from a few thousand people and the noise and the tumult on the floor to an office by yourself. Here you're just looking at a few screens and the only sound is yourself banging your head against the wall when you're wrong. It's a different kind of environment.

Q: *You mentioned preparation.*

Larry: That's essential.

Q: *In what way does Larry Rosenberg prepare himself for the next day's trade?*

Larry: I play with a number of systems, different averages that I use. I use specific averages for different markets. I find some are particularly effective in certain markets. And that's a wonderful thing about a computer; it can do all the work for you so quickly. You can put in the data and back test. I won't use anything unless I've back tested. I try to determine an established trend, and then I use my averages for timing, for entry purposes going with the trend.

Q: *Do you buy breaks or buy breakouts in the market.*
Larry: All of the above. It depends on what the market is doing.

Q: *So it changes with market conditions.*
Larry: Absolutely. Markets and market conditions.

Q: *Right. What do you feel is the key to a successful day trading system?*
Larry: Honestly, I think if you're day trading, assuming you have a market that's moving a market that's in a range, you can almost flip a coin—heads, you buy; tails, you sell—and if you have proper money management and good risk control, you will make money.

Q: *Believe it or not, we have seen some computer studies that show exactly that.*
Larry: Oh, I believe it.

Q: *Random buys and sells over a period of time using proper money management will make money.*
Larry: Sound money management, that's the key.

Q: *Bob Koppel and I have told people at seminars that there are times when you might have a series of 20 losing trades in a row, and that's where the confidence in the system has to come in because, as you know, most traders won't take the 21st trade, the one that may, in fact, become the start of a long series of winning trades.*
Larry: That's very true. I had to learn that coming off the floor. If your system works, you're going to pick winning trades 60 percent of the time, and even 50 percent is wonderful. I mean, that's just wonderful! But we also know that doesn't mean, necessarily, that you make ten trades and five or six of them are going to work. It's over a period of 100 trades or 1,000 trades. So you have to have the belief in yourself and the system and hang in there.

But that also involves money management. You can't overtrade your position. I mean, you have to be mindful of whatever percentage of equity is at risk and have the stop loss in place. And if you stick with that, you'll do fine. Of course, it's easier said than done.

Q: *How do you personally deal with the losses?*

Larry: Well, I'm not a good loser, but you have to deal with it. I guess it's like being a prize fighter, and, you know, if you go in the ring, you're going to get hit. Mike Tyson gets hit. He doesn't lose, but he gets hit. You must consider each loss a hit and be sure that no one blow ever knocks you out!

Q: *That's a good analogy.*

Larry: That's exactly what you have here. You're going to get whacked a few times.

Q: *Do you deal with the losses in any special way? Do you say things to yourself?*

Larry: I like to run. If I get beat up in the market, I can get in a real bad funk. I'll take a few days off, go out of town, go skiing, go fishing, do something. You know how it is; I go just to get my mind off trading. I find physical activity—working out in the afternoons or running—is the best thing for my head. But you have to deal with the feeling in a constructive way. That's the game.

Q: *There are many people who don't think that day trading is possible. You and I know many traders who are successful at it. Why do you think day trading intimidates so many traders?*

Larry: For obvious reasons. I think people often get stuck looking at only one or two markets, and when those markets become range bound, it's very difficult to make money. You have to be able to diversify. That is difficult for many people. Also, it requires a lot of preparation and quick decision making.

Also, people are always searching for reasons for the market's movement. To hell with reasons! The only reason

I need is the tick marks. What the market's trading. That's reason enough for me! This type of thinking is difficult for many traders.

You can read all the fundamentals you want afterwards, but if you're trying to day trade, you absolutely can't get your head messed up with fundamentals. An opinion will lay you away. Just watch and respond to the market.

Q: *What do you think are the essential differences between long-term and short-term trading?*

Larry: Well, one factor is patience. If you're a position trader, you have to have a lot more patience than if you were a day trader. By the way, that is something else that took me a while to learn. I mean, as a floor trader, the rule is instant gratification. I used to say, "Don't confuse me with the facts. I don't want to read anything; just let me react to the market." Now, as I suggested, that still holds true if you're day trading. You don't want to get into fundamentals and all the numbers; just trade the market. But as you go longer term, you have to really exercise patience and possess some fundamental understanding of the market. Day trading is different. You establish parameters. You enter your trade, put in your stop and basically you're on autopilot. I don't mean to be redundant, but all these actions assume discipline and good money management.

Q: *When you day trade, is the day isolated in your head, or does it have some relationship to what's taken place, say yesterday or the day before or to whatever time frame might be important to you?*

Larry: When I day trade, I kind of stretch it out a little. I don't necessarily get out at the end of the day. I may take home a winning trade. On the other hand, today I traded the currencies. What came before was of no importance to me. I just reacted to today's price action.

Q: *How do you deal with profits?*

Larry: I think that's a good question. I find it's much easier to take a loss than capture a good profit. When you establish a trade, generally you know where your loss is. You're willing to accept that. Off the floor, taking profits is hard to learn. I always try to take a partial profit. Psychologically, it's important to do so.

It's really a cliche: Let your profits run. I've never really known what the hell that meant. But it's an ideal, and it's very, very difficult to do. That's why I said earlier that now that I'm off the floor, I have some profit objectives at all times for that reason. I kind of watch how the market acts around that level. If it stalls a little, I will at least take some profits; but in truth, I've found that taking profits is more difficult than taking losses. More fun, but more difficult!

Q: *It seems to me that there are more decisions that have to be made when considering profits. People shy away from making too many decisions; they're afraid that they're going to make the wrong one—that they're getting out too soon, for instance.*

Larry: Well, that's how you learn. I think every decision in trading is just a learning experience. That's how I learned, really, to become a better trader. I'd be right and end up with 25 percent of what I should have. I'd say, "Well, okay, you don't beat yourself up over that." It's the same with taking a loss. You use the experience as an opportunity to learn. I think that's the attitude you have to assume to be a successful trader. I do want to make another point. I think a lot of people get involved in day trading because they think it doesn't require the overnight exposure. It doesn't require a lot of capital, and they are not at all psychologically suited for it. Day trading is something that requires total concentration. If I'm day trading, I don't want to be talking on the telephone about the Blackhawks game or, you know, the last book I read. I mean, I'm totally focused on day trading and nothing else.

Q: *It's a job!*

Larry: You bet it's a job. I think a lot of people who are new to this business come to day trading, again, because it's not as capital intensive, but they're not equipped for it. They're really novices at the business, and I don't think a novice really should be day trading, for the most part. I think it's difficult. You'd have to start off maybe short-term trading, but I think you have to become comfortable with the market and proper order, entry and stops before you get into day trading.

Q: *How important is focus?*

Larry: It's absolutely important. That's what I'm talking about. Because of the compressed time frame, your level of concentration has to be laser straight. It's not like the people who make two or three trades a year. If they close their mind down for a few days, it isn't going to hurt. If you're day trading? Take your eye off what you're doing and it may mean failure instead of success.

Q: *Don't confuse day trading with day dreaming?*

Larry: Yeah. You just lose the whole flow. You get out of tune. I guess I'll go back to the fight analogy. When Mike Tyson is coming at you, you don't want to be looking away!

Q: *If we had to talk about the optimum state of mind for day trading, what would it be?*

Larry: I think you have to be—you should be—energized. I get that by running. You have to be focused, centered. Some people do that with discipline, meditation, things like that. I mean, whatever works for you. You must be totally concentrated on what you're doing and feel relaxed. I mean, if you're going out drinking all night before coming in here to trade, you're dead meat. I think you have to be conditioned, physically and mentally. Just like an athlete. You have to come in relaxed, rested and energized; save reading the sports page until after the market. In short, treat it as a real job.

Q: *What recommendations would you give to people who are currently having difficulty day trading?*

Larry: The markets have been very difficult recently; that's no secret. But I think if you're having difficulty, I'd look at some of these things. I'd say, "Look at your work today. Have you really put a full day's duty into it? Are you using good money management? Are you trading the right markets for day trading? Maybe you should shift and trade something else."

There are some markets I don't bother trading no matter how good they are. The reason? Because I know it just isn't suited to my own temperament. There's no rule that says you have to trade everything, and sometimes you lose focus if you're looking at too many.

Q: *When you are day trading, what time frame do you operate in?*

Larry: It all depends on the market. For some markets, I'll use an hourly or 30-minute time frame. Anything less is just too much noise. I rarely go under 30 minutes. When I started, I tried five minutes, but I soon gave that up!

Q: *What I have found so interesting in writing this book is the wide variety of successful day-trading approaches. One of the ways is to catch a lot of moves in markets that are fairly volatile, like S&P's and currencies. Another way is to make a decision in a direction on entry and exit point, and that would be it for that particular day and market. Which way do you approach it, or do you use a combination of the two?*

Larry: I'm probably somewhere, not quite in the middle. I'm probably more towards the latter. I tried the one, where you had a lot of things just jumping around and moving. It just wasn't that comfortable for me. I always felt like I was somewhere, off base. I'd rather be focused on one market in which I can identify opportunity. I think if you try to stay in tune every day with ten markets, it just isn't going to work, and I think you're just trying to dance between the raindrops. A person can make a lot more the other way. You can make a lot more trading less and catching more moves, making more thought-out, reasoned trades.

Q: *Is there any specific methodology or approach that you use that you have found to be particularly suited for profitable day trading?*
Larry: You wouldn't believe it, but what I do is really very simple. Very basic stuff! I use simple trend lines, congestion areas and hourly highs and lows. It's amazing. Some of your basic stuff like chart formations, channels are incredibly profitable.

Q: *The proof seems to be all in the doing and not in any particular method?*
Larry: The basic stuff works. You just have to be able to jump in and manage the trade.

Q: *Any recommendations for people who want to get involved in day trading?*
Larry: Well, I think for people who are thinking about day trading, it's a business. It's a skill. It requires learning and practice. You cannot treat it as a part-time thing. You know, you wouldn't start a dental practice and begin to drill teeth. You wouldn't go to a dentist who drills teeth part-time. It's the same thing with trading. Also, you have to develop your own style. Do not rely on market letters that tell you to buy here, sell there. It's OK to read them; maybe you'll get an idea. In fact, some of my best trades were made by taking the opposite trades of so-called market experts. So you must develop your own technique and style. And like I said, I've spent over 30 years floor trading, and it took me a couple years to learn how to trade in front of a screen. It requires patience. It isn't going to happen in a week or two.

But when it does, you'll love every minute of it!

CHAPTER 10

Toby Crabel

William H. (Toby) Crabel is a long-term trader and market analyst. He has been a floor trader and wrote a newsletter that market professionals closely followed. Mr. Crabel has done extensive computer testing of short-term price patterns and is the author of the book *Day Trading with Short Term Price Patterns and Open Range Breakout* (1989). He is currently a Commodities Trading Advisor.

Q: *What really works for you in day trading?*
Toby: It's hard to say, but what I've come up with recently is a shorter-term system, with a lot more discipline than I've had in the past. I think that is the most important thing in any trading approach. You have to create rules for yourself and then follow them. The funny thing about it is that the rules aren't objectively set out for you. They're not real clear cut; there are a lot of bromides, but there's nothing necessarily definite that works for you! You test

the common wisdom, and it doesn't work or works in a particular context, all of which is not necessarily what you need. So what is truth and what isn't are very difficult things to pin down. I think the whole process of getting to where you need to be in trading is finding out what the proper rules are that work for you. It has to be coordinated by testing, at least in what I do—especially in day trading, because the edge is so elusive. The essential thing is defining the rules for yourself and then following the rules so you have a standard to judge yourself by. I think that's the key ingredient.

I know one thing for me is that, in order for me to make money—the more outside pressure I have, the harder it is for me to trade. I think the only way you can sort of circumvent that is to make it systematic. That's for me. I don't think that's true of everybody, because I sure meet some really talented systematic traders or discretionary traders who do really well, much better than I've ever done in my career. So I guess what I'm saying is that I'm a man with severe limitations, and I'm having to work pretty hard to work with what I have to try to figure out how to counter those limitations and stay at this business and profit. How long has it taken? It's still going on.

Q: *Right. It's a process—it's a work-in-progress, right?*
Toby: Absolutely.

Q: *What about some of the early experiments? What were they like?*
Toby: I've seriously looked back to some of my early experiments. Every once in a while I'd run across an idea that just worked extraordinarily well. I'd trade well with it, and then I'd start losing money, because someone would get on to it, and that would kind of be the end of that. And then, I'd look again, I'd find something that worked, maybe more sophisticated, took more of an education on my part, and then I'd implement it. That would work for a while, and then it too would stop working.

Q: *And why do you think that these things stopped working?*

Toby: I think it's the nature of the market. I used to think of the market as a physical mechanism that we could measure—just like anything in physics. I thought of it like a plutonium world, but that was dead wrong. And it's a dangerous assumption to make, because what we're really dealing with is human beings that have free will. And at any moment, they can catch on to what's going on in the markets and change their behavior. So basically I had to re-orient the way I thought about the market in some very fundamental way.

You see, I believe the key is to find something that will work over the long run, and then implement it so you can use it and make money.

You want to get a very basic idea and trade it a lot of times over a long period of time with small amounts of money. That's gambling theory, I think, more than anything. You want to become like the house. You have an expectation for profit, and you do it a lot of times. In other words, you beat your cost a lot of times, whether it's just barely or a lot. You can do very well if you beat your costs a thousand times.

Q: *Why do you think that so many people have difficulty with day trading?*

Toby: Day trading itself has difficulties. I mean, there's an element of randomness within the day time frames, especially now because of the push and pull that goes on with the large CTAs (Commodities Trading Advisors) and pool operators. They come into the markets with large orders. And there's a tremendous push and pull that goes on in the short run. That creates a lot of problems for a day trader. Now it used to not be that way. I mean, we can run a simple test, for instance, and look at trendiness based on an expanding day's range with a close in the bottom 10 percent of the day's range and an open on the top 10 percent of the day's range, and vice versa. If we looked at it over two to

145

three years and compared it to the two to three years prior to that, I think you'd find many, many more trend days occurring back in the early '90s or late '80s or even in the mid '80s than you do right now. And the inter-day time frame isn't as trendy as it used to be. So if whatever you're doing depends upon trend, you're going to have some trouble. You're going to have to make some big adjustments to trade effectively. So what the inter-day time frame requires you to do is make adjustments constantly, more than any other time frame. You're constantly having to adjust your systems because of the changing nature of the market. Remember, you can make money day trading! But I think making money day trading is more difficult, much more difficult, than the longer time frame.

Q: *Do you think day trading is the most difficult kind of trading?*
Toby: Absolutely the most difficult. The shorter the time frame, the smaller your expectation, the higher your cost, the greater your slippage in commission! That about sums it up, doesn't it?

Q: *Yes, but it's being done successfully in many quarters, and we know that there are some advantages in terms of risk parameters and capital utilization.*
Toby: Yes, of course, but if you're looking at it as a possibility, you have to be aware that the shorter the term you get, the higher the costs get, the higher your slippage gets, the more difficult it becomes, essentially. And you have to factor that in. Now I think those are very clear-headed evaluations of what you're up against as a day trader.

Q: *What about the psychological aspect?*
Toby: Well, if you're discretionary in your trading, and you're day trading, you're almost like an athlete. You have to be very fit physically. You have to be extremely aware. You're going up against people who are incredibly quick and bright. You're really going into the most competitive area, and then you're also subject to the whims of CTAs,

and CPOs (Commodity Pool Operators) and the hedge fund managers. So you're subject to their vagaries, and that's always an extremely unpleasant thing to be up against.

So to sum it up, you have to be incredibly nimble as a discretionary day trader and incredibly smart. Now there are people out there who are both of those things, and then the issue is that you have to have a great deal of stamina to keep it up. You also have to know what your limitations are. If you are going to perform well in this very competitive arena, you're just going to have to be at the top of your form along with everything else.

I used to sell a daily letter to floor traders, and one of the things I noticed about floor traders is that, if they had to work as hard as they do in the first hour of trading all day long, they'd probably last only three months or something. The exertion of effort is just incredible!

Q: *What do you think is the optimum day trading psychology?*

Toby: I think you have to know where you are in the time frame you're trading, as a day trader. You've got to know that you're going to have to expend tremendous amounts of energy, not as much as a scalper would if you were doing high-intensity work all day on the floor. But you just need intensity and the ability to pay very close attention to what's going on.

Q: *The intensity of scalping is both physical and emotional.*

Toby: Absolutely. I think the shorter your time frame, the more energy and effort it takes, the greater the psychological demands are.

Q: *But you know what? I think those psychological demands are just as strong in people who are trading off floor.*

Toby: Yes, I agree, I mean, especially the discretionary trader who's day trading. I think the primary job is watching every tick and being alert for any new upcoming movement or any changes in the environment.

Q: *Could you describe your current day trading methodology?*

Toby: My methodology is mechanical now, so I've found I can be somewhat clearer on the expectations of a discretionary trader. I tried to go through that for a long period of time and found it to be very wearing. It took much too much energy.

Q: *Does your computer generate numbers?*

Toby: It's totally automatic. Now I say the machine tells me what to do. I developed the program.

Q: *Of course.*

Toby: But the machine pretty much monitors the market, and it tells me when I have an indication.

Q: *And is it based on anything that people would recognize, like moving averages or overbought, oversold or oscillators or something familiar?*

Toby: Overbought/oversold is I think a good concept. Also I think, depending on how you define it, I use a sort of a mix of the momentum, which is a short-term trend following indicator, and what I would call a reversion type system, where the market may be going up, and you're selling.

Basically I'm looking at two concepts: short-term momentum and short-term reversing. Those are the two broad categories of trades that I have in the portfolio.

Q: *How did you arrive at this method?*

Toby: I read some studies of price moves off of the opening, and although these studies weren't very systematic in their presentation or analyses, they showed some promise, that markets tended to move in a direction after it moved off the opening range. It has been around forever; it's an old floor trader's trick. You know, locals tend to fade early moves, but if there's a surge off the opening of some quality, it tends to continue. I must say, I found a lot of interest and possibility in this.

Q: *Right.*

Toby: I mean it's a very real, clear example of behavioral change that takes place, because people are getting wise to an idea, a tendency. So the basic idea is taking a move off the opening. I think you have to modify it, but in general, I think this is a piece of market behavior that's going to continue to work for a long time.

You know, it's the irony of the markets that I think you have to be prepared for. You have to be prepared for your system not to work for a long time and know that what you have and what you're trading is general enough and basic enough so that it will work and weather the storm.

Q: *How do you deal psychologically with the losses?*

Toby: When you're doing really well over a period of time, I think there's a tendency to get lazy, maybe overconfident. Even as a systematic trader, your day-trade execution may not be quite as sharp as a result of that. And I think it shows. You know, you may be nodding off when a single comes, for instance, because you're so comfortable with your recent home run. I think that's a real common thing.

Q: *Do you get concerned after a series of losses and start looking to tweak your system?*

Toby: After a certain point, yes I do. And that's why I think that this is an ongoing process, and I think it's always important to try to improve what you're doing. You always have to ask yourself if what you have is reflecting something that is truly capturing what the market is doing, what the market's reality is, for lack of a better phrase.

Q: *Does it become a confidence issue?*

Toby: Well, after, I have certain limits that I impose on myself, draw down limits and things like that. If I reach a certain point, then I start to seriously question what it is I'm doing, and of course, I won't tolerate a draw down of more like 4 percent or 5 percent from a peak on a daily basis.

If you don't make money for long periods of time, there's certainly something to question. The market is a great teacher, and if we pay attention we learn from it. If things aren't going well, I think it's probably a good time to be doing research. It certainly seems like it's a lot easier to do research when you're losing money! But it's important to remember that the research pays dividends and lets you move beyond the period of losing.

Q: *What about profits?*

Toby: I think you train yourself to be extra alert. When I'm profitable, I'm looking ahead at price objective and becoming somewhat apprehensive, about draw downs.

To some extent, I've reversed the natural human inclination to get excited when I'm profitable and to get depressed when I'm not. This has been helpful.

Q: *I would assume it's very helpful to even out the emotional states and stay on an even keel, to have some emotional equanimity about the whole process win or lose.*

Toby: It's baffling for anyone observing who doesn't truly understand. When I'm profitable, I just tend to never let myself get too excited about it. The key is to try to retain some sort of even keel throughout wins and losses—that's the better approach. Of course, it's a very hard thing to do.

Q: *It certainly is.*

Toby: How do you do it? Well, it's one of those basic questions. It's personal. Each trader has to deal with that in a very personal way.

Q: *One of the initial ways to deal with it is to recognize that it's an issue that requires attention. Many people ignore it.*

Toby: I think the longer you're at it, the more you're going to look at the emotional side of trading. I've got a family; I've got people I care about. Now, I'm not going to take a mood swing based on some random event in the market. I'm not going to jeopardize these relationships. It requires recognition and commitment. I go out and play a lot of chess or take a long jog. I know people meditate and do things like that!

Q: *Yes, we tend to hear a lot about that.*

Toby: I think there's clearly a physical element that is associated with stress and anxiety that you can dissipate easily with some activity. I think it was something I was reading that made that point. I think it was written by, let me see, Bob Koppel and Howard Abell.

Do I remember reading somewhere that trading is not aerobic by any means because we're sort of sedentary and concentrated? It's an intellectual process, and there's a lot of stresses that aren't necessarily dissipated. Physical exercise is an excellent thing to balance out the stresses that go along with trading. As you know, particularly with something like day trading, where each day is its own little microcosm, it would almost seem a necessity to have some physical activity going on in life. You need to get in some aerobic exercise to dissipate your anxiety. Look at a longer-term trader. Imagine being involved in a trade that lasts four or five months. The days are certainly not nearly as intense as a day trader's.

Q: *Well, there are a lot fewer decisions to make.*

Toby: Absolutely. As a day trader, you'd probably want to go out to get aerobic exercise a few times a week just to keep yourself in top form.

Q: *I think that has a lot of truth to it. Why do you think most people are unable to day trade successfully?*

Toby: I think a lot of people get into this business, and there's a lot of wishful thinking. They see something that really isn't there—an easy way to make money! I think it's one of the hardest ways in the world to make money.

I might add, I think there's a tremendous amount of literature out there that's wrong and is misleading. It creates more problems than it solves, especially for people who are just starting out in the business.

Q: *What kind of literature?*

Toby: You know, trading systems, books on trading. I think that it's real easy to get bad information. It's an industry—books written by people who don't have a clue. I think I should say that your work is very good, but you guys are real traders.

Q: *Yeah, that is one of the secrets.*

Toby: You see, the real secret for success is that it's a lot of hard work, and if you want to do this over a long period of time successfully, then you'd better not think about going in and making a lot of money fast. The common idea is let's make a big killing and quit.

Q: *As you know, Bob and I have written about this, and I think most, if not all, of the traders we've interviewed have recognized that if there's any secret or Holy Grail attached to success in our business, it comes from within. It has nothing to do with any specific indicator or system. It has to do with how you perceive the markets and operate within that context of your own psychological makeup.*

Toby: I think you're absolutely right.

Q: *And if there's anything that we're trying to do, it is to remind people that they have to understand the inner workings of themselves in order to operate in the day trader's environment.*

Toby: I totally agree with that.

Q: *What recommendation would you make to traders who are currently having difficulty with their day trading?*

Toby: Well, first you have to be sure that's what you want to do, day trade. It's a major life decision! It's different from other forms of trading, and you've got to know what you're up against. You're competing against some rough, tough competition. So that's one thing I would suggest. I would also suggest not to take it too personally because of the difficulty involved. Just understand that the time frame that you're asking yourself to do well in is the toughest time frame in the world for a trader. It's the toughest time frame there is in trading.

Another piece of advice is that if you want to do it on a consistent basis over the next ten years or something like that, I would recommend trying to do it systematically. I know, again, there are exceptions. I think that to the extent that people follow a method and follow rules, they can do very well. Someone not doing well in a day time frame, or any time frame for that matter, is the one who can't really face the reality of the game or manage what they're doing well. And in the short time frame, in the day time frame, things happen very quickly, and decisions have to be made. If that isn't automated, if there isn't some sort of at least internal automated process, they're going to have a lot of difficulty when the going gets tough. So I would say, if it's not going to be systematic, then automate it as much as possible and set the rules that you're going to follow so you have some standard to judge yourself by.

And I guess if you have all that down, then there's the research. I do think that once you get the basic rules down and the approach—not that you can't change those and improve them—the research on market action is extremely important. A beginning trader, after a year of really rigorous research, can learn an awful lot about the markets, much more than someone who is just watching the market and not taking good notes. It may take five years. The research can really get you ahead of the curve, and I think that that's extremely important. And once you've learned a method and have an approach that works, you've got to stick to it.

Q: *It's all execution, isn't it?*
Toby: Yes, execution is key.

Q: *I think you've made a really significant point that even traders who are discretionary must systematize something in order to deal with the chaos of the market. And of course, once* *they systematize whatever their method is, they have to actually do it.*

Toby: You know, in the final analysis, we have to look at ourselves and ask: Can I do this? Do I believe in what I'm doing, and can I actually implement it? But you know, there's nothing like a good statistics course, a lot of reading about market action and a good programming course, if you know what I'm saying.

Q: *Yes, that's the systems trader in you coming out.*

Toby: Well, these are all tools that will help you to get at the insights a little bit quicker.

I think this is a real entrepreneurial business, and it demands that you be extremely well rounded.

Q: *But again, what good is the best system in the world if you don't use it? One other thing: Take up jogging!*

CHAPTER 11

Mei Ping Yang

Mei Ping Yang is Vice President of Foreign Exchange Trading for Goldman, Sachs & Co. in New York. She specializes in the currency markets.

Q: *Can you describe your basic day trading approach?*

Mei Ping: Basically I have one particular approach to day trading. When I say "day trading," I want to specify that my day trading tends to be my particular trade at the beginning of the day or even the middle of the day, ending only at the end of the day. My trade tends to occupy one whole day.

Q: *What kind of system do you day trade?*

Mei Ping: It is actually a very basic five-wave system: I try to enter at the end of the second wave and just hang on for the third to the fifth wave.

Q: *Well, that's not bad.*

Mei Ping: It's a very basic approach, nothing fancy, because I hate to do anything too fancy for short-term trading. As I said, it is very basic. If I can't see the trade, I'll just let it be!

Q: *Has your trading gotten much more complicated as you've evolved as a trader, or has it stayed pretty much the same?*

Mei Ping: I have always looked for a very self-contained method simply because I always believed that if I can't explain it to myself very quickly, then I don't really want to get involved with the trade.

Q: *Do you ever take an overnight position?*

Mei Ping: Yes. But when I do the short-term stuff, I usually am in just for that session.

Q: *You mentioned that your system is fairly basic. Is it essentially counting Elliott Waves?*

Mei Ping: There is that and just basic chart patterns. Typically, I narrow it down to five-minute charts, just basic bar charts, where I can count the waves, as I've said.

Q: *What do you think is the key to a successful day trading system?*

Mei Ping: To just concentrate on that particular pattern and not worry what will happen after that; not to worry what will happen after the pattern is over, and make sure that you take your profit when the pattern has evolved.

In currency trading the five-minute charts are good for 30 ticks. So you must pocket the money. If you get greedy, however, the five-minute chart will kill you.

Q: *So you can't be greedy with a very short time frame.*

Mei Ping: That's the discipline. The moment it hits your level, and the fifth wave is finished, just get out!

Q: *Right.*

Mei Ping: But sometimes it seems like the five is having a failure. You get out too soon.

Q: *I think I ought to say for the benefit of our readers that your primary interest is trading the currency markets that can have a lot of volatility and move enough to trade on a five-minute chart. There are other markets that may not trade with as much volatility. However, you could still day trade them but not so much on a five-minute chart.*

Mei Ping: Exactly.

Q: *I mean S&P's, of course, is the classic five-minute chart that I think that everybody uses. So in a sense, what you're saying is this: The key to the successful day trading system would be not to be too greedy, pay attention to the time frame that you're trading in and stick to your particular point of focus.*

Mei Ping: Yes. Stick to your pattern and time frame. I think what is most important is that the trade is an automatic reflex, that you just have to do it, and your stop has to be there. And for me, when your fifth wave is up, take your profit. Don't say, "Ah! Let's go to a bigger time frame," or follow the larger daily or weekly trend.

Q: *Yeah, that's a no-no, isn't it? Why do you think that so many people think it's impossible to day trade successfully?*

Mei Ping: I think a great deal depends on one's temperament. Personally, I found it very seductive, because you just do it and you go home and you're done with it. The other side of it is that in day trading you constantly have to monitor the screen, which, if you do not want to do, is not an ideal situation. It requires a great deal of attention and intensity.

Q: *A great deal of concentration and focus.*

Mei Ping: Right.

Q: *Like a real job.*

Mei Ping: Exactly.

Q: *You know, I think that a lot of people tend to feel that there's something romantic about day trading.*

Mei Ping: I think, as I said before, it comes down to a matter of personality and temperament. It's more of my own personality. There are some people who are very good at day trading and continue to do so and, in fact, hate to do positioning trading.

Q: *What do you think is the proper psychology for successful day trading?*

Mei Ping: I think in day trading, especially, if one is not feeling well, one shouldn't really do it. You must be at your best to be effective.

Q: *What about your frame of mind?*

Mei Ping: That's really more of what I meant. If one is feeling bummed out, short-term trading is not to be done. Sometimes not being in the right frame of mind makes you feel bulletproof.

Q: *And what do you think the optimum trading psychology is?*

Mei Ping: I don't think about the past or future. One has to be very "present" is what I'm trying to say. You must trade in the moment.

Q: *In the Zen present.*

Mei Ping: And stay loose enough to watch for the opportunity and, when the opportunity comes, to not think about it but to just trade it.

What I'm trying to say is that it's very important to always keep an eye on other things at the same time you're focusing on your market, particularly when day trading. So for me, it means knowing what's going on while I'm watching my bar charts and the five-minute entry points.

Q: *How did you develop the basic approach?*

Mei Ping: It just evolved, simply because I was noticing how these little five-minute things seem to be the clearest picture of five waves. I could see five waves on five-minute charts, but I'll be damned if I could see them on daily or even weekly charts. Now isn't that interesting?

Q: *Well, the experts insist that they're there.*
Mei Ping: Well, as long as I cannot see it, then I don't trade them!

Q: *Right, but they're there on the five-minute.*
Mei Ping: For me, they're obvious.

Q: *You know, it's all a Rorschach test anyway.*
Mei Ping: Yes, I know. I think what happens is a function of that. The way I look at it, some other people might say, "I don't see it," and for them they are completely invisible.

Q: *Well, that's good. I think one important point that you're making is that everybody has to believe in what they see and operate only on the basis of what they see and not what somebody else might see.*
Mei Ping: That analysis certainly works for me.

Q: *I think trying to use other people's methodologies and forcing them to fit your personality often hurt people.*
Mei Ping: I know from experience this is true.

Q: *And along the same vein, I know that you can't have a winner every single time you trade. So there must be some times that you take losses.*
Mei Ping: Oh, yes. I know about that.

Q: *How do you deal with those losses?*
Mei Ping: There are times when you have several losses in a row, and you just say, well, statistically I understand the loss in terms of my system.

Q: *What do you say to yourself then?*
Mei Ping: I think, at this point, I have enough confidence within my system that I just assume a certain proportion of trades will not be winners.

Q: *Right.*
Mei Ping: I remember recently I was having a string of losses and I said, "Okay, let me stop trading for awhile," simply because after a while I began to lose my focus. I just

159

had to stop a while, take a break and then cool off, so I could be fresh again.

Q: *And when you came back?*
Mei Ping: When I came back, I started small. You take your profit faster. Do what has always worked for you in the past so you can rebuild your confidence.

Q: *It is always nice for one's psychology to take profits.*
Mei Ping: Yes.

Q: *Speaking of profits, how do you deal with the profits? Many people, as you know, have as much difficulty with managing the profits as they do with taking losses.*
Mei Ping: Yes, of course. People say to themselves that these profits are too good to be true, and then they go out and self-destruct.

Q: *Self-sabotage?*
Mei Ping: It's all personal demons. I have my own rule for dealing with this. If, after my first, I allow half or more of my profits to whittle away, I stop trading for the day. The reason is obvious: So that at least half of it still stays there.

Q: *And then you start up again the next day?*
Mei Ping: Yes.

Q: *You get out of the positions?*
Mei Ping: Yes, and the discipline is not to do anything.

Q: *With the idea of starting the next day with a fresh mind?*
Mei Ping: Yes. It's a little rule that keeps you safe. It protects yourself from yourself. It's just a basic money management rule.

Q: *Speaking of money management, do you have a specific money management formula?*
Mei Ping: For me, it's very intuitive. When I start the day, I just begin with my normal position and then just make sure that the amount I trade is appropriate to the market condition. I am always aware of what I should be

losing. If I make a lot of money, then my trading size may increase a bit. If I lose money, then, of course, my trading size will decrease accordingly.

But for me it's more than intuitive. It also depends on the time frame I am trading in. I think it's all a matter of expectation. If I don't expect a retracement, then I'm in trouble—then I know I'm in trouble, and I should get out! But if that back and fill is within my scope of expectation, then I know it's going to test. But I don't want to miss the move either. Then it's all right for me, psychologically, to risk the loss.

I might not be very happy if I give up profit, but psychologically, at least, it is within my specific expectation, which means I can take the trade with equanimity. However, if I'm not expecting the loss, then it's much harder for me to allow that position to get into trouble. I might just try to break even, if nothing else.

Q: *So what you are saying is that, from your point of view and method, anticipation of the market is very important.*

Mei Ping: There are times when the market is kind enough to go exactly according to the script that you've written, exactly according to your expectation where you have anticipated correctly.

Q: *That's right. That's the most comfortable feeling, isn't it?*

Mei Ping: Of course, it is the most gratifying, but I think one should never get into a trap and say, "I'm invincible," as a result. So I try not to do too much of that. I just let the market tell me what should happen. My responsibility is to stay focused and respond appropriately.

Q: *Do you set specific objectives on the trades you take?*

Mei Ping: It's more like when the market swings back, I consider how far back it will move.

Q: *Right.*

Mei Ping: So I just let the swings control my expectation.

Q: *So you monitor the swings, and if the swings become excessive, that's information.*

Mei Ping: Right. I should watch the market unfold.

Q: *Why do you think most people have difficulty day trading?*

Mei Ping: I guess the concentrated time frame makes it very difficult for them to deal with profits and losses.

Q: *What recommendations would you make to traders who are currently having difficulty with their day trading?*

Mei Ping: I'd ask them to really make an effort to understand their personality makeup, to really be able to answer the question: Do you know yourself? If you do know yourself, then I think it's much easier to figure out a specific trading strategy to be successful in day trading.

Q: *There are some people whose temperament is absolutely ill-suited to day trading. They are just not constitutionally able to handle the psychological challenge.*

Mei Ping: Personally I always believe in pushing the envelope of what one is. I think, in order to do that, one must have the luxury of being able to do that. And if one has the ability, then it's better to know what is easier for one and then just go with it, rather than to struggle with every part of the process.

Q: *Right.*

Mei Ping: I guess what I'm trying to say is: If you don't know your own personality, then I think you shouldn't be trading in the first place—day trading or long-term trading. And of course, as I've said, day trading in particular makes many more psychological demands on the trader.

Q: *So first we look into ourselves?*

Mei Ping: Right. But more importantly understand ourselves.

Q: *Right.*

Mei Ping: Because trading is going to tell you about yourself, an awful lot about yourself, isn't it? In fact, trading is an inward journey to who you are.

Q: *From a tactical point of view, what do day traders have to do differently in your opinion?*

Mei Ping: I think day trading must be more automatic. People who cannot operate in a very automatic way and who have a tendency to second-guess themselves will have problems. You have to be very sure of yourself. So tactically, you must have all this in place before you trade.

You also have to be happy with this time frame, doing the same thing day after day, seeing the same thing and working with the same markets. For many people, their level of interest won't sustain an excellent result. It becomes very repetitive, and they lose intensity and focus.

Q: *What final words of advice would you offer to an aspiring day trader?*

Mei Ping: I'm afraid this will come out wrong, but I would say that day trading is better than any narcotic.

Q: *It is better than what?*

Mei Ping: Than any narcotic. I know it's a very incredible way of looking at things. But it can be such a rush, so exciting. What I'm trying to say is that if you have a good day trading system, you just must be able to operate so automatically to be really, really good. It requires focus, concentration and intensity. You have to be in a charged, positive state of mind.

Because the slippage is unforgiving, you can't twiddle your thumbs. You have to grab every opportunity. You can't hesitate; if you do, the market will hurt you. That's all I'm trying to say. It can be very exciting if your psychological temperament is well suited for it.

CHAPTER 12

Bob Koppel

Bob Koppel is President of Innergame Partners, a proprietary trading and trader execution services division of LFG, LLC., a Chicago-based FCM clearing all major world exchanges. Mr. Koppel is the coauthor with Howard Abell of *The Innergame of Trading* (Irwin, 1993) and *The Outer Game of Trading* (Irwin, 1994). He is the author of *The Intuitive Trader* (Wiley, 1996). Bob was a long-term member of the Chicago Mercantile Exchange, where he traded successfully for his own account.

Q: *How long did it take you to come up with a day trading approach that worked for you?*

Bob: I've been trading for nearly 20 years on and off the exchange, and it's taken every bit of the 20 years to develop the skills that I use on a daily basis to trade markets. There's no end point in becoming a successful trader. It's a process.

Anybody who's serious about trading and who truly wants to become successful at it has to realize that there's no room for complacency. You really never get to a level where you say, "Hey, I know it all." And if you ever get that feeling, then I would suggest to you that it's a symptom to be very concerned about. So to get back to your specific question, it's something that I work on, on a day-to-day basis, and you know, there are obviously certain strengths that I've been able to cultivate over this period of time. But you know, there are also some soft spots, and I work on them on a daily basis. It's part of holding that mirror up to your face.

Q: *What was the learning process like?*
Bob: Like most things in life, even if you're lucky to have a natural talent for something, talent is usually not enough. Trading requires a lot of discipline and hard work and a commitment to develop whatever natural endowment or ability you might possess. Quite frankly, I found it very difficult, in the beginning—particularly being on the floor. As you know, my younger brother preceded me as an exchange member by about five years. When I started in the business, he was already highly successful at trading, he handled rather large numbers and he was a known personality on the trading floor. I think that just exacerbated my initial frustrations. I started off trading just one lots and continued to trade them for over a year with mixed results. I guess that first year I was just looking for anything that would work consistently.

Q: *Can you talk a little more about your experience?*
Bob: I think the operating word here is "consistency," because during that first early period, my goal was not to make money but just not to lose it. I was just trying to learn as much as I could and develop something that was consistent. That takes a lot of work.

There would be days that I would make a lot of money; there would be other days when I'd give it all back and more. So I had to figure out something that was consistent. One of the things that worked for me was to figure out a way to eliminate the emotion when I traded markets. The way I did that was by being able to identify what I thought were major points of support and resistance in the market, and I would wait to exploit opportunities in the market around these points.

If the market was having a big rally, came into an area of major resistance and began to slow down, or if I could see some of the smaller locals becoming big buyers and getting bullish at these major points of resistance, it would be key information that this was a point to begin to consider the short side and to operate in the same fashion at points of support. I found this to be a very successful technique because it produced consistent results. The tough part, however, was when I was able to identify these opportunities to take action, because it's one thing to be able to find something that works consistently and it's another thing to be able to consistently use that technique. It took a lot of years to be able to work on the psychology of trading so that I could act absolutely automatically without any emotion at all as I trade now. If I see something, I just absolutely go for it! The discipline is to consistently take these trades no matter what. No emotion, no fear, no complacency, just pure action free of any resistance.

Q: *Has your approach changed as a result of your move from trading on the floor to off the floor?*

Bob: I think the approach that I use now, in broad strokes, is not very different from what I used on the floor. It's true that you have a lot more stimuli to work with when you're on the floor because, of course, you can see the locals. You know who they are. You work with them day in and day out. You understand what most of your colleagues' points of vulnerability are, what their thresholds of pain are, where they're willing to give up. I used to look at very subtle things. I would watch people and monitor the flushed color of their skin. I would look to see if they were swallowing a little too hard. There are lot of things to go by when you're trading on the floor that are more difficult to apprehend when you're off the floor. But in essence, what I try to do, once I identify a market that seems to hold some opportunity, is to acknowledge where this market has been. Even when I'm day trading or trading a 30- or 60-minute time frame, I really want absolute, complete familiarity with that market. I want to know what that market has done over the last six months. What has it done over the last six years? What has it done over the last six days, and what has it done over the last six minutes? And once I factor all that information in, I try to figure out in my own mind what is the current position of that market. When I talk about position in that market, I mean is that market at a point of accumulation? Is it at a point that is in the main phase of that market? If it's an up market, is it in the main phase of a bull market, or is it in the last legs of the bull market? Is it going through a period of distribution? And that will determine whether I'm more likely to buy a break or buy a rally or sell a break or rally. If I feel a market is at a point of accumulation, I think there's a lot of potential on the upside. I am certainly not going to sell a break in that market. But even if I feel the market has a long-term bullishness to it, if I feel it's at the last end of the bull market, I might be much more likely to sell a break in that market than I would in an accumulation phase. So these are all the sorts of things that I'm looking at. Additionally, my personal point of focus is the internal architecture of the market. I'm always trying to determine—based on the last move of the market—the last swing on a weekly or on a daily basis, the next probable retracement of the market. And of course, you never know the exact answer to that question. Based on probabilities, if a market has a tendency to retrace 50 percent over a rather long period of time, has now extended to a point and looks like it's going to pull back a little bit, I'm going to certainly acknowledge the importance of a 50 percent retracement. In general, that holds true for most markets, but the difference has to do with what is the particular personality of that market. As you study charts, you'll see that some markets have a very natural tendency to retrace 50 percent; some have a natural tendency to retrace 30 percent from a big move; and some have a natural tendency to retrace 60 percent. Those are all considerations that I factor into my trading equation.

Q: *Can you talk about some of the methods you have used over your career?*

Bob: Over a 20-year career, I've tried many things. Being a voracious reader, I try to keep up with everything that comes out about finance or trading. How does that Cole Porter song go? "I've been through the mill of love?" Well, I've been through the mill of trading books and subscribing to other peoples' hotlines and faxes and buying software. I've done it all, and what I've found is that all you really need is a method that works well for you, a method that can give you consistent results and is appropriate for your personality. That's the key to the treasure chest!

Whatever strategy you use has to be right for you. I've read all the books, studied different trading systems and pattern recognition, and just really tried a lot of different things. Many of those systems and books, in the long run, were of no value. Upon further reflection, their real contribution was in making me realize that you have to go it alone. You have to find out what works for you. So ironically, those books and failed systems proved to be highly instructive and useful.

Q: *What do you think is the key to a successful day trading approach?*

Bob: I think the key to success to any trading approach is really quite simple. The first part of it has to do with having a system that works consistently. When I talk about "system," it can be a method, an approach. It could be intuitive. It can be your ability to trade by feel in a way that is consistent over time. That's the first part of it. The second and most important part of it is to have the kind of psychology that will allow you to operate that system effectively. Day trading is infinitely more difficult than long-term trading, and that's why most people who write about trading talk about how difficult it is to have a successful result at day trading. The key to day trading is learning how to deal with the losses. There are a lot of losses because of the compressed nature of the trade. It really requires that you come in and out of the market many more times than in a midterm or longer-term method.

Q: *Do you think that it's possible for people to day trade successfully?*

Bob: Yes. However, it requires a different set of skills than long-term trading. Day traders have to be in a position where they can make multiple decisions about entering and exiting markets all the time. What makes it very difficult is that it almost seems like you're always lost in the noise. To be successful in trading in general, you have to be able to distinguish between what's essential, what's the signal, and what's just the noise, what's the "ground cover," if you will, of the market at any given time. And because of the nature of short-term trading, it seems as if most of the time you're caught up in the noise.

You really have to have a methodology with which you can consistently approach the market and look at it through the lens of what's really critical. It can be a retracement method. It can be a method that's based on strong support and resistance. It can be a system that's based on moving averages. Or a system that's based on nonlinear indicators. You do need something that will allow you to make that distinction between the momentary emotion of the market and the real value. And that is infinitely more difficult to do as a day trader. However, saying that, if one does come up with something that works, day trading can be enormously rewarding: There are many homes built on the North Shore of Chicago that are the result of day trading profits. So it can be a very profitable and intellectually rewarding enterprise, but like anything else, you have to find something that works. And the key is that it has to work consistently over time.

Q: *What do you think is the proper psychology for day trading?*

Bob: Clearly, from my perspective, psychology is key. After you find one method that works, it's all psychology. Day trading feels like you're constantly taking a roller coaster ride on emotion, and guess whose emotion that is? It's your emotion! You have to know how to deal with that. You have to know how to deal with that feeling of not being able to get into the market. You have to be able to deal with that natural fear of giving up profits.

Psychology comes into play in a very critical way. As you know, one of the things that I bring to the attention of traders is that we all have these natural psychological biases. If you can remember back to the time you were in college and took Psychology 101, the instructor showed examples of various optical illusions. The point made was this: The way that we are created genetically as human beings predisposes us to possess certain natural perceptual biases. In fact, they are perceptual distortions. The way this is usually illustrated is by presenting a number of famous illusions. We've all seen these illusions, the Muller-Iner Illusion, the Tichnor Illusion and Helmholtz Illusion. The most famous one is of the two parallel straight lines, one with contracted arrows at the end and one with extended arrows at the end. The instructor would ask which is the longer line. Of course, the line that had the extended arrows appeared to be the longer, but as a matter of fact, both lines were exactly the same. It's our perceptual bias that makes us see one line as longer and the other as shorter.

The biases that we bring to trading are of a psychological rather than of a perceptual nature. So there's some very strong psychological biases that we have to learn how to overcome. I usually talk about four: (1) a bias for certainty, (2) a bias for control, (3) a bias for avoiding pain (losses) and (4) a bias of believing that the way we see reality is a reflection of the way things really are.

The first one, which has to do with certainty, is a very important one, and it's a bias that every trader should over time learn how to deal with effectively. We have this natural belief that in order to trade effectively, we have to know everything. And of course, the key to trading is that you can never have complete certainty. I mean, nobody in the world can have all the available information about any given market. I used to tell this anecdote that there were two people in the world who truly understood all the fundamentals in the gold market, all the factors which determined the true value of gold: One was long and the other was short. The point is that no one can ever really have certainty about a market, and as a day trader you must understand that.

The complication, on a psychological level, is that even though you can never have certainty, you must act as though you do have certainty. You have to act from a feeling of certainty and confidence. The key, of course, is to realize that you don't need certainty. It almost sounds like a Zen koan. When you realize you don't have to know, you will really know. But the only way you come to that realization is if you wrestle very diligently with the whole issue of certainty. How much certainty can you ever have? I mean, everything might line up perfectly for you in terms of technical analysis for, let's say, the British pound, and it looks like the very best sell in the world as a day trade. There's nothing that indicates to you it's the wrong decision. You might have a major support point in your favor. You might have the moving averages in your favor. You may have ADX in your favor. You have the statistics in your favor. Everything lines up, you have certainty and it is the best sell in the world. And then George Soros decides to buy 100 million British pounds. Throw your indicators out the window! You can never have certainty!

The next psychological bias that you have to overcome is the one that involves control. You cannot control the market. And this is very difficult for many traders to grasp psychologically because almost everything else, in order to achieve success, involves some kind of control or manipulation. We tailor the external environment to gratify our image of it. We do this in terms of who we are, what we look like, where we live, who we associate with. We're constantly manipulating the external environment to suit some internal vision that we have of it. You can't do that in trading! You cannot control it. The only way you get control is by realizing you don't need control of the external environment. The only thing you need to be able to control is your internal impulses to be able to get over internal resistance and be able to effectively act upon your system.

The other natural psychological bias that I spoke about was the natural aversion to pain or, in the case of trading, to taking losses. We all naturally hate to lose, but in trading you must lose in order to be successful at it. So you really must understand that losing is not incidental to the whole; it's absolutely to be expected. It's an eventuality in trading, and it's the one thing that all great traders share in common: They know how to lose. So that's another, natural bias to learn how to overcome.

The last one is really the most difficult one. It's in a pure sense a psychological issue and has to do with one's own belief system. The more you trade and the more sophisticated you become about trading, the more you realize that all you're ever really trading is what you believe about yourself and what others have socialized you to believe about yourself. So you really have to hold that mirror up to yourself and say, "Hey, this is what I believe about myself. Some of these beliefs are really going to make me a great trader, but other beliefs that I possess will work against a successful result."

You know, the trader might believe that he doesn't know enough or he doesn't have enough capital. Hell, he might be right! He might want to sell the market but fear that someone like George Soros is going to be buying it. Or he might feel he doesn't have certainty, and that he absolutely must possess certainty in order to trade. Or he might be afraid to take a loss. Remember, to succeed at trading, you must take a loss, and you must assume loss. A loss is not accidental or incidental to the process. It's a necessary and natural by-product to trading. If you're going to trade well, you're going to have to take a lot of losses, and you're going to take more losses in short-term trading than in long-term trading because of the compressed nature of the time frame.

So all these factors about what that trader believes about himself will either accelerate his progress, or it will drastically inhibit his performance with disastrous results.

Q: *How do you handle a string of losses?*

Bob: As I suggested before, nobody likes to lose, but you have to be psychologically prepared to lose in order to trade effectively.

Loss is a very complicated issue. You know, I often laugh to myself when I read trading books. You can go through a 300-page trading book on a particular, technical-analytical method, and nowhere in those 300 pages will you see the letters L-O-S-S. And that to me is a very strange thing because loss is so key to trading! Maybe they should be calling this whole process "trading-losing" because losing is such an integral part of trading. It really doesn't separate out.

All the great traders understand how to lose. They know how to embrace risk, and they know how to embrace loss. They know also that if their loss is well managed and circumscribed, no loss will get out of hand. Whatever action they take in the market, win or lose, over time, as part of a much larger trading process, will have a successful result. Hey, you could write a book about this! I have.

Q: *What about profits?*

Bob: As complicated is the issue of loss, taking a profit is much more difficult. There are a lot of people who can buy at a certain point and put a stop loss order in. But when they get a profit, they're so quick to capture that profit that they never allow the trade to grow into its full fruition. The key, I think, is to understand how markets are driven. I mean, this is a cliche, you know, that we've heard time and time again: Markets are driven by greed and fear.

In my view, markets are driven only by greed; it's just that the manifestation of that greed comes out in the form of fear and hope, you know, fearing that you're going to lose and hoping that you're going to win. The problem, from a psychological standpoint, as it relates to trading, is that most people are manipulated by those two emotions in a way that is injurious to a positive trading result. Most times when somebody's in a trade that goes against them, they start hoping or wishing that the trade comes back. Therefore, they take a much larger loss than they normally would take if they had the risk well circumscribed without that feeling of hope. On the other hand, when the trade starts going their way and gratifies their initial perception of the market, they start fearing that they won't capture all the profit that is in that trade at any given point of time. The fear manipulates them to get out of that trade too soon.

What I've found very successful is to try to discipline myself to reverse those two feelings as they occur in me while I'm trading. At this point it's almost automatic when a trade starts going against me: I see fear, I hear fear, I feel fear, and I get out of that trade immediately. I will not stay with that trade one more nanosecond than is necessary, because I fear that the trade's not going to work out, given my technical parameters. I don't want to wish or hope it comes back; I want to be manipulated by the fear that I'm wrong, because I'm wrong a lot!

On the other hand, when the trade is going my way, I want to not allow fear to get me out of the trade until it gets to a point where I think it's appropriate to take profit. So the emotion that I allow myself to experience at that moment in time is hope or faith—or belief might be a better word—in my technical ability to allow that trade to grow into its full potential.

Q: *Why do you think most people are not as successful as they want to be when they attempt to day trade?*

Bob: I think the fear of losing is a very strong factor, because when people start losing in trading, the loss becomes much more than just a trading loss. There are all sorts of psychological associations that people make with losing. If someone is not of the temperament to day trade, she might take three or four or seven trading losses in a row and suddenly recall what Uncle Harry said about her, "she'd always be a failure." These emotions start overwhelming us, and these associations of past failures and past losses in a psychological sense start making us associate our trading losses with who we are as individuals. It can be very negative and very deleterious both on a psychological level and in terms of having a decent trading performance.

Trading is very much like athletics. Just think about the psychological state of mind that you have to be in to be effective at sports. Remember the time in your life that you really excelled in some athletic event, and think about your psychology at that time. What was your state of mind? How were you feeling? Could you have a great result as an athlete if you're feeling lousy? Can you perform terrifically well on the football field if you have this perception of yourself as being a slouch and a loser? It couldn't happen! The same thing is true about trading. You must discipline yourself to be of a state of mind that will result in top performance all the time. It requires a lot of hard work. You really have to work on yourself more than you work on the markets. But hell, you must know the markets. You must be totally cognizant and familiar with whatever you trade. You must do your homework. This is not a game for wannabes. You're going against the very best minds in the

world. But having said that, doing all the technical analysis and all the intellectual preparation that trading requires are not enough. You must be of a psychological mind and an emotional temperament that allows you to play the game full out. You cannot play not to lose; you must play to win all the time.

Q: *What recommendations would you make to people who are having difficulty in day trading?*

Bob: The first thing, and it is going to sound obvious, is that you must believe that you can make money day trading. There are many people who do very well on a consistent basis week in and week out, month after month—they make money day trading. You must believe that's possible. If you don't believe it's possible, clearly you shouldn't be trading. That's the first belief you have to have in place. The second belief that you need to possess is this: You have to believe you have a system that works. And the way you get a system that works is by finding a method that works consistently over a long period of time based on a proven methodology with sound money management and based on sound probability theory. And you must test it. In a statistical sense, you must determine that there's reliability to that system. That's the second thing you need in place.

And the third thing is that you must work on yourself. You must spend as much time working on your own psychology as you work on your charts. Now for a lot of people, that's a totally abstract concept. They think, "Hey, why should I work on myself? All I need is a trading method that works. All I need to do is become familiar with my chart." All the fine technical analysis in the world will not help you overcome your fear of trading and all the other psychological fears and anxieties that we've spoken about.

So there are three things: (1) You must have a belief in place that this entire enterprise of day trading can and will result in a successful outcome; (2) you need to develop

your own trading method that works; and (3) you have to work diligently on yourself on an ongoing basis.

It's like working out. You can't work out just once and assume you're going to have good muscle tone; you've got to be committed to doing it as a continuing process. The good news is that trading is incredibly rewarding. Not only do you learn a lot about the markets; you learn about yourself. Some things you don't necessarily want to learn about! But I will tell you this—you're greatly enriched by the experience both financially and psychologically if you have what it takes. Trading is the ultimate trip, but you need the right temperament and have to be willing to pay the price. It's a high price. It's a painful price. But my God, it's the best thing going!

CHAPTER 13

Newell Stevens

Newell Stevens (pseudonym) is a long-term member of the Chicago Mercantile Exchange. He is a principal of a clearing firm that specializes in the proprietary trading of agricultural products. He is one of the leading players in the agricultural sector of the Chicago Mercantile Exchange. Because this is his first public interview, he has requested anonymity.

Q: *What is your basic approach to day trading?*
Newell: Well, to begin with, I deal with a long-term philosophy and an outlook. I trade off of that philosophy and outlook, but I don't continuously hold positions for the long term. In other words, I'll put a position, and I'll trade off of that position. I may trade all or part of that position at any given time if I feel the market in the short term is out of line. It is a risk management technique I developed so that I don't have to experience the drawdowns of long-term trading.

Q: *Could you be more specific?*

Newell: Let's say I'm trading the long side of the market, because I'm bullish. I may take profits, but then I'll buy them back higher if need be, if I don't get my positions back where I want them. For example, I'm long-term bullish, and I buy a market at $40; I think the market is going to $50, but if I get a quick run to $44, I'll take some profit. I'll buy them back again on a moderate setback or buy them higher if need be. If I hear something in the fundamentals or perceive something in the action of the market that makes me leery, I'll get out of the market on a short-term basis. It's very intuitive. I do it on feel. If something doesn't feel right to me, I'm going to get out. I will not sit and hold any position if I'm uncomfortable with it.

Q: *Even though you have a very strong intellectual conviction about the fundamentals in a particular direction?*

Newell: Yes. If I hear something short term that I don't like in the market action—I'm a believer that the market's always right—I'll get out because I say to myself, I sure wouldn't be getting in here. So if I wouldn't be getting in, it's a good place to get out. And I'd not only do that for me; I'd do it for my customers. And they have to pay full dues. But long term has made me successful and made my customers good money. I don't worry about the commission.

Q: *But one of the fears that most people have about doing some of the things that you do is the fear of not being right, and of leaving money on the table because they don't get in. Do you have a built-in methodology that gets you to reenter the market?*

Newell: Yes, but I never worry about that. In fact, sometimes you're right. I won't catch the whole move, because I have to get in and out, or sometimes I'll catch more of the move, because I'll get out and the market sets back. The markets set back, and I get in better than where I got out. In truth, it doesn't bother me. As I said before, I'll buy them back at a higher level, if need be, if it looks like I got out and I shouldn't have. It doesn't bother me at all. This method has proven to be highly successful over a very long period of time.

Q: *Did you always trade with this approach?*

Newell: I've traded all different ways. But this has been the most successful way for me. I have tried to just put it on, let's say, a long position and not move. But that method, even when I have good location, never served me best because, as I said before, I don't like sitting through the setbacks. In fact, what my system allows me to do is turn the eventuality of these setbacks to my advantage. So that's how I use the day trading to maximize my long-term outlook.

Obviously, if the market just keeps going in my direction, I'll ride it for as much as I can get out of the trade.

So the essence of my method is this: I'm using the day trading to just catch the natural movement of the market moving in the direction of my original expectation. I'm watching the short-term movement, looking for a good place of entry. If the market starts acting heavy on me, no matter how good the news is, I'm getting out. This way I can give the market a day or two to rest and then, if things change, get right back in. It doesn't bother me if I'm getting in higher or lower.

Q: *You're really using the day trading as a way of playing the natural swings of the market.*

Newell: If I'm looking for a $10 move in the hogs—many times hogs move in $10 swings—I may be in and out of that market 30 times or more!

Q: *And you might even make $15 on the trade instead of the $10.*

Newell: Exactly or maybe catch only $7 of it.

Q: *But you'll feel more comfortable with that approach. Do you use any technical indicators since you're primarily a fundamentalist?*

Newell: Yes.

Q: *Any secrets you would like to share?*

Newell: No. I really don't have any. As you pointed out, I'm a fundamental trader, but I'm always aware of the technical aspects of the market, especially moving averages and that type of thing. But that's about it. I may look for technical price objectives.

Q: *You are a fundamentalist who day trades. Are we to believe it's possible that you don't need an arsenal of highly sophisticated technical indicators?*

Newell: I don't look at those things. I look at the moving averages. The ten-day averages in the hogs. That's one indicator that gets me out. The market tends not to extend from the ten-day averages on a big run. It tends to come back and try to test those averages. So I kind of watch them. That's about it. As I said when I started, I trade short term from a long-term philosophical approach.

Q: *What do you think the difference is between your approach and someone who is a pure long-term trader?*

Newell: I think most long-term fundamentalists don't monitor the day-to-day news as closely as I do. But from my perspective, that has been the key to my success. I monitor the news almost hourly, and I tend not to discard information that will have a short-term impact on the market.

Q: *It's interesting that you not only pay attention to the inter-day noise, but you have learned how to capitalize on it and always see the forest for the trees. It's pretty unique.*

Newell: I'm a short-term, day-to-day fundamental news trader.

Q: *And yet you're always aware of the overall market situation.*

Newell: That's right. I have long-term objectives. I have a three, four, six-month view. I'll be in and out of the market dozens of times. Now I should add that probably the biggest reasons for me to trade this way is the size of my positions. I pile a very big position on, and I tend to either be in it or be out of it.

Q: *You're either right or wrong for a large number.*
Newell: Generally speaking, I'll put on my whole position at one time. If I'm going to buy 700 or 800 contracts, I'll buy them right away and get out of them the same way!

Q: *And the day trade is made all on "feel"?*
Newell: Yes. It used to be that you could trade 1,200 to 1,500 contracts that way. Now the market won't handle that many. Some days it will when the market gets to running, but I would say, because of the current structure of the market, I can't trade as big as I used to.

Q: *But the concept's the same.*
Newell: Yes.

Q: *What is going through your mind just before you put your position on? Do you have a dialogue with yourself?*
Newell: Yes.

Q: *About what?*
Newell: Monitor, I keep telling myself. Monitor the news. If, for example, the market knows the news, is it reacting right? How does it feel?

Q: *If you think the market should open lower and then start to rally but doesn't, you're gone?*
Newell: Yes. Say the news is good, and they're calling the market higher. Maybe it should be 30, 50 higher or something like that, and the market opens steady lower. I don't like that at all because it means a lot of the buying is already in the market. I do the same thing with markets I don't know as much about.

I know much more about the livestock than I do the grains, but I trade them the same way. I trade very large positions in the grains. I do it exactly the same way. I'm either in them or I'm out of them. I don't have any special knowledge of the grains that everybody else doesn't already possess—so I watch the action, to see if it reacts the way it should. Anytime it gives me a hint by the way it feels that I should bail, I'm out.

Q: *You mentioned that you trade the same way for your clients?*

Newell: Yes, I do exactly the same things. I trade my customers exactly the same way. The way I look at it is this: As long as I'm making them money, somebody else is paying the commission. I always ask them to focus at what they've made at the end of the year, the percentage they've made on their investment.

Q: *How do you feel about those times that the market tops out a little bit, and it opens 100 higher the next day? How do you deal with that psychologically?*

Newell: I have no problem with that. Oh, I mean, like everybody, you'll have a little bit of a regret, but no big deal. In fact, I've done that and bought into the market at 100 higher. I've put the market 100 higher the next day just getting in. That does not bother me one iota. If I don't like the feel, I'll put the market down. Everybody says, "Well, you're destroying the market." Well, no. I'm doing what the market's telling me, and I just put it limit down. It's not at all about me. When it's right to buy, I just buy; and when it's time to sell, goodbye!

Q: *So in a sense, you're really committed to the idea that you're going to be very disciplined. When it is time to get it, you're just going to buy the market.*

Newell: It doesn't matter to me.

Q: *And when you're wrong?*

Newell: The same way getting in or getting out.

Q: *But doesn't the fact that you're looking for short swings affect your entry? I mean, you're going to pay 100 higher.*

Newell: Well, I think the market is going to make another leg up.

Q: *The beginning of something much larger than just that little one- or two-day swing up?*

Newell: I'm assuming there is another leg up. But again, remember I'm using the short term to my advantage.

And I've calculated that the market can handle the size of my position.

Q: *What would you tell someone who would try to emulate your style?*

Newell: If you take on that philosophy, then you've got to take your profits and losses the same way. Too many people like to trade the short term, and they turn losing day trades into positions.

Anyone can take a profit; it's knowing how to take a loss and knowing when to take it. I mean, a lot of times the market moves against you. Sure, you should be adding to the position, because it's still right, and it's giving you a chance to add to it at a better level.

Q: *When it moves against you?*

Newell: Yes. Sometimes that's the time to be adding, but you've got to know. As long as I still feel that my conviction is right and there's something extraordinary that's causing it to be out of whack a little bit—and not so much just the action—then I'll go ahead and take advantage of it and add to the position. But when a market all of a sudden just fails, I will get right out. To be able to make these distinctions obviously takes years of experience. Trial and terror!

Q: *Do you ever use a computer program for entry points?*
Newell: No, never.

Q: *All decisions in the market are based on what you're "feeling."*
Newell: Exactly. And then so much of it again is predicated on my long-term outlook and what the market should be doing given the short-term news.

Q: *It pretty much comes down to this: Does the market feel right or wrong to you? What recommendations would you make* *to someone who is interested in being a successful short-term trader?*

Newell: If you're going to trade short-term, for short-term profits, make sure your losses are short. That's the biggest one. Trade exactly that way. I do!

Q: *So the losses have to be small.*

Newell: Yes. I'm not saying profits and losses should be the same amount, but your thinking has to be the same. If you go to trade for short-term profits, then you've got to trade your losses for short term.

Q: *Do you prepare the night before?*

Newell: Hey, you can't just sit there and pray for winners!

Q: *Yeah, right.*

Newell: Too many people hope, you know, pray. Wish. Dream. Look back. You just can't do that.

Q: *So a lot of what you do, essentially, is intuitive—you respond to the market action to give you clues.*

Newell: Yes and the market news.

Q: *Do you think you're preparing or approaching the market differently than somebody who looks for a longer time frame?*

Newell: Oh, absolutely. I think part of that stems from the fact that I have been on the floor. And by being on the floor, you tend to trade shorter term. So many of the other people that trade longer term do so because they're off the floor. Now I'm off the floor, but I still keep the same mentality of a floor trader. I think that's probably it as much as anything.

Q: *You know being on the floor doesn't mean you were a scalper.*

Newell: Yes, of course, but people who paid their dues on the floor have a mentality. I very seldom even trade on the floor anymore. I trade my customers with the same mentality as I trade myself, which would be similar to a floor trader.

Q: *How do you use charts?*

Newell: I'm not good at reading the charts. Even so, I don't put a lot of credence in them. I look to see where they've been, where they look like they might go. I look more at the averages, kind of where the average is, and so you see where the money is, who's got the money. Is it with the bulls or the bears? That's about it!

Q: *Do you ever find people who have good ideas but can't execute them?*

Newell: Can't trade them? Absolutely. They can't trade their way out of a paper bag and yet have a good feel for and good thoughts for a market. They can't trade at all.

Q: *What do you think prevents them from doing that?*

Newell: Not everyone can be a trader. They just don't know how to pull the trigger. They just can't. And it may not be money; they may have all the money in the world, but they cannot trade. Hey, this is not an easy thing to do. As I said before, there's a certain mentality.

Q: *Yeah. It doesn't have to do with money.*

Newell: You and I both know some of them and can name them. They will have good ideas but just can't trade.

Q: *Right.*

Newell: Or they'll have the idea, and by the time the market starts to move in the manner they're saying, they're starting to reverse themselves already. No, I know people like that. I'm sure you do too.

So it comes down to this: You can have an idea, but you have to take action. You can have the risk control, but you must be able to pull the trigger to get the whole process underway! This is not for everyone. But if it's for you, you'll wake up each morning with a smile on your face!

PART FIVE

Winning Versus Losing

CHAPTER 14

How Winning Day Traders Think

I have had the good fortune over a long career to have the privilege of calling many of the industry's most prominent traders friends. I have chosen to include below a sampling of top traders' thoughts about successful short-term trading.

This sampling of traders includes individuals whose experience covers every aspect of the futures industry. Some have owned and operated their own clearing firms and have had the opportunity to mentor many traders during their careers. One trader has 40 years of continuous trading experience, and the others average about 20 years. Each is successful trading for himself or herself and/or for others.

I think their perspectives give real insight into how their minds work and why they are able to trade with such success.

Joseph Siegel

According to Joseph Siegel, "All successful trading comes down to three things: knowledge, nerve, and the ability to lose money.

"Everybody has the ability to lose money, but it takes nerve to lose and then choose to stay in the game . . . to want to come back . . . to have the audacity to assume that you're smart enough to make your trade and take advantage of opportunities and make money. I found that the psychology of being able to lose money and come back was a big factor, because it's very easy to lose money and very easy to become discouraged. You have to have a great deal of confidence in yourself that even though you've taken a beating in the market, whatever form it takes, you can come back, you can return and trade effectively.

"Any trader would greatly benefit by learning how to teach himself or herself to become more confident. Confidence comes from a belief in oneself based on hard work and disciplined trading. Do not overtrade! Start slow, work your way up and don't be jealous of the other traders; it makes no difference what the others are doing! If you learn to understand yourself, you've got an edge on everyone else."

Gene Agatstein

Gene Agatstein observes: "Successful trading gets right down to the psychology of self-esteem and confidence. If you're trading long enough and intensely enough, I think ultimately the statistics have to work in your favor—if you just hold on to the winners and cut the losers. So why doesn't it work for everyone? The answer is *self-confidence*."

George Segal

George Segal puts it this way: "I think that successful traders have a personality, that they're not afraid to have 19 losing trades out of 20, because the 20th can be a trade that's much greater than all the 19 put together. They're not hung up on losing money. They want to protect what they've got and wait for the opportunity to make a lot of money.

"They're willing to accept the loss, to take a loss and come back and make another trade, and know there's always tomorrow. There's always another trade to be made tomorrow. They don't like to take a big loss.

"There are also people who are afraid to go into trades, but they shouldn't be trading if they're afraid to get involved, even if it's only one lot. I mean, I would assume many people have gotten out of trading because they're afraid to make trades."

Linda Bradford Raschke

According to Linda Bradford Raschke: "My philosophy is to do whatever works, whatever makes your bottom line go up.

"My number one job is to make a living, not to be a millionaire overnight. I've got to put bread and butter on the table, pay my bills. I've got to make a living. This is what I do for my job, so I need a steady, consistent equity curve. That's why I try to concentrate on the shorter-term time frame. I just like the comfort in small, steady gains.

"Another thing I want to emphasize that you learn, whether you trade short term, from a mechanical system or a methodology like what I teach: *It's important to be consistent.*

"Trading is just a numbers game, that's all it is. You get a little bit of an edge in your favor, a little bit of an arbitrage, a little bit of a price pattern. Anything that gives you that edge. But you have to have that edge. And then it is just a numbers game. You crank that out; you say I've got to do 100 trades, with 65 percent winners and 35 percent losers. That's my average loss. You have to get that consistency going. If you're consistently losing, then maybe it's time you get a different pattern, a different edge or an arbitrage. So you have to look at the long-term scheme of things.

"Even though I look at my profitability every day, I'm not necessarily looking at each and every trade.

"Just because I am a short-term trader doesn't mean I don't hold trades for the long term, too. Believe me, I have put on a position and stuck with it for three months. I just don't look at the thing. I have to take it off my quote machine, off my trading sheet, out of my mind, or I'm going to want to play with it. It's like those seasonals. They drive me crazy sometimes because, even though they work, I'm looking at this position and I know I'm supposed to leave it on for another three weeks, but I want to get in there and start fooling with it.

"So work with what fits your style. On the trading floor, we're constantly scaling in and scaling out of trades. That's one of my big money management things now. I'm always scaling out of things. Put yourself in a win/win situation. Take some money off the board. Take partial profits. Because that way you can't lose. If it goes against you then, at least you locked in something. If it goes your way, you still have bullets to play with. Don't get greedy.

"You have to define what works for you. There is not anything wrong with one time frame or another; or one style of trading or another; it is all a little road map in my head. It teaches me to anticipate, to have a plan. I watch it set up; if it's there and it is doing what I expected, I'm in the trade."

Donald Sliter

According to Donald Sliter, consistency is the key to successful day trading: "One of my goals is to stay disciplined. Another is not to allow myself to get lazy. My goal is to trade every day. It's my job. I consider myself a blue-collar worker with a white-collar income. Would you believe I have not had a losing month since November, 1986! Each day I just chip away. It has gotten to the point that they're not all little chips anymore, but I still view it as chipping away. To other people the numbers are awesome. I've watched the guys who hit the home runs, and you know it's just not my style. I don't like putting all my eggs in one basket. I don't believe in that!"

CHAPTER 15

Principles of Successful Day Trading

Principles of Successful Day Trading

- Define your loss.
- Believe in yourself and unlimited market possibilities.
- Have a well-defined money management program.
- Don't buy price.
- Don't take tips.
- Don't trade angry or euphoric.
- Trade aggressively at your numbers and points.
- Focus on opportunities.
- Consistently apply your day trading system.
- Be highly motivated.
- Don't overtrade.

- Never average a loss.
- Take small losses, big profits.
- Have no bias to either side of the market.
- Preserve capital.
- Think in probabilities.
- Always trade in a highly positive and resourceful state of mind.
- Act in certainty.
- The market is never wrong.

Trading presents many challenges, but as with most things in life, persistence and patience, confidence and competence and, above all, a willingness to pay the price will give you the desired result.

In *The Mental Game*, James Loehr, writing about tennis strategy, observes:

> Many players believe they must do something very special and different on big points. As a consequence, players often break from the pattern and style of play that got them to the big point. Going for too much too early is a strategy breakdown. Going for the low-percentage winner is particularly tempting on the critical points (to get the high-pressure situation over with) but generally spells failure.
>
> Another common way of breaking down strategy-wise on big points is to suddenly start pushing the ball back, hoping your opponent will make an error. Shifting to a very conservative, unaggressive style on the big points in order to keep your errors to an absolute minimum will be about as effective as going for too much too soon. The old dictum, never change a winning game, still holds. Whatever you did to get to the big point, continue doing. As a general rule, you

will be most successful if you learn to play offensive, high-percentage tennis on critical points. You become the aggressor and work to get your opponent to make a forced error, without making an error yourself.

To do this, you must know your own game well. Your general strategy for big points should be worked out well in advance of your match, and breaking down is when you don't follow it.

This analysis is as true for trading as it is for tennis. In fact, trading could be called a state of mind, an exciting and challenging contest that is deeply satisfying and financially rewarding. Some top traders view it as an art form like bonsai or the martial arts. And as in these art forms, trading requires its own discipline in the form of appropriate goals, attitudes and strategies.

Bottom Line

Now ask yourself the same question all serious traders must ask themselves: Do you have what it takes?

As you think about your answer, consider the positive beliefs held by the top traders.

Positive Beliefs of the Top Traders

- I believe I am or will be a successful trader.

- I believe I can achieve excellent results in my trading.

- I believe I can identify and execute winning trades.

- I believe I can trade with confidence.

- I believe I can trade effortlessly and automatically.

- I believe each day's performance is fresh.

- I believe I am personally responsible for all my trading results.

- I believe I can be successful without being perfect.
- I believe my performance as a trader does not reflect on my self-worth.
- I believe one bad trade is just that.
- I believe trading is a process.
- I believe that by believing in myself and in any proven methodology and by approaching trading each day with a fresh, positive state of mind, I possess the ultimate trading edge.

Trading is a rewarding universe of unlimited possibilities when approached with maturity and well-managed risk. It is intellectually challenging and affords independently minded individuals the ability to participate in a personally fulfilling and profitable activity. Day traders can and do consistently make money.

Success in trading!

FOR FURTHER READING

Barach, Roland. *Mindtraps: Mastering the Inner World of Investing*. Burr Ridge: Irwin, 1988.

Baruch, Bernard M. *Baruch: My Own Story*. New York: Holt, Rinehart and Winston, 1957.

Douglas, Mark. *The Disciplined Trader*. New York: New York Institute of Finance, 1990.

Gann, W.D. *How To Make Profits Trading in Commodities*. Pomeroy: Lambert-Gann, 1976.

Koppel, Robert. *The Intuitive Trader: Developing Your Inner Market Wisdom*. New York: John Wiley, 1996.

Koppel, Robert and Howard Abell. *The Innergame of Trading: Modeling the Psychology of the Top Traders*. Chicago and Cambridge, England: Probus, 1993.

Koppel, Robert and Howard Abell. *The Outer Game of Trading: Modeling the Trading Strategies of Today's Market Wizards*. Chicago and Cambridge, England: Probus, 1994.

Le Bon, Gustave. *The Crowd: A Study of the Popular Mind*. 2nd edition. Atlanta, Ga.: Cherokee, 1982.

Schwager, Jack D. *Market Wizards: Interviews with Top Traders.* New York: New York Institute of Finance, 1989.

Schwager, Jack D. *The New Market Wizards: Conversations With America's Top Traders.* New York: Harper Business, 1992.

Sperandeo, Victor with Sullivan T. Brown. *Trader Vic— Methods of a Wall Street Master.* New York: John Wiley and Sons, 1991.

INDEX

Howard Abell is Chief Operating Officer of Innergame Partners, a proprietary trading and trader execution services division of LFG, LLC., a Chicago-based futures clearing member (FCM) clearing all major world exchanges. He is the coauthor, with Bob Koppel, of *The Innergame of Trading* (Irwin, 1993) and *The Outer Game of Trading* (Irwin, 1994).

Innergame Partners have trained hundreds of traders from around the globe including many floor traders who are currently active on the Chicago Mercantile Exchange, Chicago Board of Trade, and Chicago Board of Options. Innergame Partners have 40 years of combined experience as exchange members where they traded successfully for their own accounts. They currently manage the Innergame Trading Portfolio.

For additional information about their brokerage or informational services, please contact:

Innergame Partners
30 South Wacker Drive
Suite 2720
Chicago, IL 60606
312-715-6102
800-664-1852
312-715-6133 (fax)

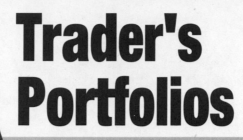

New
CD-ROM Money Maker Kits
from Dearborn Multimedia

Features:

- **25 minute video help with the author**
- **12-28 interactive printable forms per CD-ROM**
- **On-Line glossary of terms**
- **Quick-start video tutorial**
- **Interactive printable book on CD-ROM**
  (Print out sections you like for closer reading or writing notes.)

Start Enjoying Greater Financial Freedom
Triple Your Investment Portfolio
SAVE Thousands on Real Estate as a Buyer or Seller

Personal Finance

The Budget Kit
Create a Smart Budget That Saves You Time and Money

With this multimedia kit:
- Automate your expenses and cash flow
- Save your money for the things that really matter to you.
- Spot your actual spending patterns.
- Stay organized at tax time.
- Start enjoying greater financial freedom

Over 50,000 Copies Sold!

Order No. 1800-1301
$34.95

Judy Lawrence uses her years of experience as a personal financial counselor to show how to organize a personal budget.

Investing

How To Buy Mutual Funds the Smart Way
Find Out How Easily You Can Buy Mutual Funds and Earn Profits the Smart Way

With this multimedia kit:
- Set your own goals and build your lifetime investment program
- Discover an easy way to avoid brokers' fees and reduce your expenses
- Monitor your funds with fully interactive worksheets

Order No. 1800-0701
$34.95

Stephen Littauer has been involved in the sale and marketing of financial and investment products for over 30 years.

Real Estate

The Homebuyer's Kit
Find the Right House Fast

With this multimedia kit:
- Negotiate with confidence
- Prequalify using the automated formulas to determine your best mortgage terms
- Chart your progress using the interactive home comparison forms

Over 50,000 Copies Sold!

Order No. 1800-0401
$34.95

More than 10 million readers watch for **Edith Lank's** award-winning real estate column, *"House Calls"*.

The Mortgage Kit
Save Big $$$ When Financing Your Home

With this multimedia kit:
- Select the right loan
- Lock in the best interest rate
- Prequalify using the automated forms and checklists
- Determine how much money you will save when refinancing
- Organize your mortgage search using the interactive checklists

Over 30,000 Copies Sold!

Order No. 1800-2201
$34.95

Thomas C. Steinmetz was a senior strategic planner with the Federal National Mortgage Association.
Phillip Whitt has worked 12 years in residential mortgage lending.

Real Estate

The Homeowner's Kit
The Homeowner's Kit Will Help You Protect Your Most Valuable Asset—Your Home!

With this multimedia kit:
- Save money and conserve energy
- Refinance for the lowest rates

Just point and click to discover:
- Hundreds of home safety and security tips
- How to inspect your home

Order No. 1800-1901
$34.95

Robert de Heer is a professional real estate author who simplifies home-owning with specific money-saving steps.

Small Business

The Business Planning Guide
Plan for Success in Your New Venture

With this multimedia kit:
- Just plug in your financials to plan your dream business
- Point and click to automate planning and financial forecasts
- Start, expand, or buy a business

Over 400,000 Copies Sold!

Order No. 1800-0101
$34.95

David H. Bangs, Jr. is founder of Upstart Publishing Company, Inc.

Successfully Start & Manage a <u>NEW</u> Business